Navigation

Edited by
Inge Hinterwaldner
Daniela Hönigsberg
Konstantin Mitrokhov

Munich, 2022
Open Publishing LMU

Content

Introduction

Inge Hinterwaldner, Daniela Hönigsberg, Konstantin Mitrokhov

Users' perspectives: Dealing with JODI's %WRONG Browser.co.kr

The research project *Browser Art. Navigating with Style* examines artistic browsers and the idiosyncratic ways in which they display Internet content.[1] The project seeks to make the seemingly opaque operations of the digital infrastructure tangible and understandable. To go beyond generalized structural diagrams – which only reflect basic technical settings – this study deals with the creation and comparison of time-based portraits that shed light on the browsers' respective mode of function. Thus, the research team extends the range of analyses from the screen output perceived by the senses to the processes of program mechanics. The question of how also to preserve the endangered heritage of Internet-based art and cultural production for posterity has become an unexpected addition to the research endeavour.

The idea and experimental setup for this issue on navigation has its roots in the project and the aspect of looming software retirements which tend to disrupt art browsers as well.

Back in 2017, Adobe officially announced that it would be ending support for its Flash software at the end of 2020. While the content itself was not affected per se, major browsers would not be able to display Flash-based media out of the box from December 31, 2020 onwards.[2] This seemingly insignificant – from an everyday use perspective – and anticipated retirement of the legacy software framework is, however, obliterating access to the vast troves of artistic production that relied on this technology throughout the last two decades.

1 Browser Art. Navigating with Style, https://kg.ikb.kit.edu/hinterwaldner/2433.php [accessed 9.4.2022].

2 Cf. T.C. Sottek: Adobe Flash rides off into the sunset. It's the end of the line. In: The Verge, 31.12.2020, https://www.theverge.com/2020/12/31/22208190/adobe-flash-is-dead [accessed 3.12.2021]; Gregg Keizer: Adobe lays Flash to rest. In: Computerworld, 11.12.2020, https://www.computerworld.com/article/3601108/adobe-lays-flash-to-rest.html [accessed 2.2.2022].

Triggered by the prospect of Flash shutdown, we decided to hastily document all Flash-based artists' browsers we had on our list, in the best way we could. The task was urgent and simple: capture the browser in all its facets (as if it would completely cease to exist tomorrow) in a way that would allow posterity to get a good *impression* and *feel* of what it was like to use the software.

This rushed and 'emergency' research mode delivered some useful insights. First, we suspected there would be only rather marginal differences between our approaches. The 'best' approach is, after all, a superlative – in its everyday meaning – and how many of these could there be? However, when we compared our personal best practice documentation approaches, we were astonished at how diverse our solutions were. Thus, we decided to reflexively describe how we documented the works and why we pursued our individual paths.

Preliminary work

In our first comparative study[3] we found that different browsers shape the Internet in various ways, highlighting ever new facets yet not necessarily leading to a coherent picture of 'the' web. Browsers – like all media and interfaces – filter our view of the Internet and shape the ways in which users can intervene therein. To establish a methodological layout – as an interdisciplinary group of four researchers – we accumulated and fused our findings on five artistic browsers and analyzed how they configured the web and the access(es) to it. Here, 'the' user remained a seemingly neutral, and somewhat problematic, even generic, category.

3 Daniela Hönigsberg et al.: Negotiating the way to the Internet. On the impact of software design on browsing experience and user interaction. In: Journal Visual Culture Studies, vol. 1, no. 3, 2022, forthcoming.

Now, we would like to use the opportunity given to us with this special issue on navigation to present an experimental setup that addresses the diversification of use scenarios and users. It is generally obvious and in line with Karen Barad's theorisation that human agents are factors that impact the 'epistemic thing' (notion according to Hans-Jörg Rheinberger).[4] In this issue we would like to shed some light onto that aspect, which was previously omitted in our study.

Domains of navigation

One of the first web browsers in 1994, Netscape Navigator had 'navigation' already written in its name. It seems to be a given, to talk about accessing the information provided on the World Wide Web in terms of navigation. Indeed, this notion has been central to web browsing since the inception of the web. The concept of navigation is one of the main tenets in *Information Management: A Proposal* authored by Tim Berners-Lee in 1990, laying out the foundational structure of what would become the World Wide Web. In his proposal, Berners-Lee emphasizes the importance of facilitating navigation as a means for preventing the user from getting "lost in hyperspace"[5]. Indeed, navigation soon became reified as a navigation interface in the first web browser called WorldWideWeb. The term cyberspace[6] – understood as the Internet's infrastructure – also implies it is a space to be navigated as it shares the prefix with the ancient Greek κυβερνήτης (kybernetes) – steersman, captain, pilot or navigator, indicating a whole semantic field that spans a spectrum of meanings from 'piloting' to 'governing'. For a deeper insight scan this QR code:

4 Karen Barad: Meeting the Universe Halfway. Quantum Physics and the Entanglement of Matter and Meaning, Durham/London 2007; Hans-Jörg Rheinberger: Toward a History of Epistemic Things. Synthesizing Proteins in the Test Tube, Stanford 1997.

5 Tim Berners-Lee: Information Management. A Proposal. In: CERN, May 1990, https://cds.cern.ch/record/369245/files/dd-89-001.pdf [accessed 14.6.2021], p. 14.

6 A term famously coined by the sci-fi novelist William Gibson in 1982 in a story published in Omni magazine and then in his book Neuromancer (1986).

Our take on navigation

In a departure from the ways that designers and scholars think about (controlled) navigation and the web, we consider navigation as a mode and mood of exploring interactive software that does not take "navigational freedom" for granted. In our case study, the *%WRONG Browser .co.kr* by JODI, adopting navigation as a mode of exploration helps us to deal with a browser that overloads our sensory capacities and resists conventional attempts to capture it precisely and systematically. That is not to say that a methodologically applied navigation strategy cannot start out playfully, as trying things out and getting an intuitive idea of what the software does when we interact with it. Navigation then may become an empirical means for exploring the browser's features, bugs, static elements, dynamic patterns, and its technological environment. As such it becomes essential to our documentation approach.

Navigation in/with/on (digital) imagery

In the digital domain we are dealing with a socio-technical environment, in which some (human) actors seem to acquire a more influential, defining position than others. This is reflected in studies as they either focus on persons engaged in navigation (users piloting) or on those providing the framework for navigation (producers governing). The producers modulate navigation for the users by providing navigation tools and creating the sites in which the users navigate. In other words, digital environments are designed *for* navigation. The producers preform the navigation to a certain degree.

And, if we want to go as far as Thierry Bardini's interpretation of Douglas Engelbart's stance, simultaneously create the conforming/corresponding user.[7]

The communication studies scholar Patricia Aufderheide examines navigation along three axes: simple versus global navigation design, navigation metaphors adopted from other media, and navigation related to interactive functions, whereby: "Different navigational needs drive different navigational designs, depending on how the project construes the user's relationship with the material."[8] Here, the navigation as an aesthetic feature is carefully crafted to fit the individual project. Navigation can be bold, clear, minimalist, limited and strategically withhold information from the users.[9]

The web browser as software *renders* a website: it makes the website visible by creating an image following a specific road mapped out in the negotiation between its programming and the HTML of the accessed web page. We could say the browser's rendering engine navigates the image[10] (aka rendered websites) into existence. The digital images assembled by the web browser are not only code-based, as one would expect for digital images, they are also distributed and partially open ended or unfinished. They are gathered and composed out of text elements, embedded hyperlinks, control elements, pictures, graphics, sound, animations etc. That is why in our research we understand web browsers as 'image creating machines'.

Focusing on the image created by the browser, at least three distinct processes are performed that can be described as navigation: a) the navigation to a specific webpage, b) the navigation through the menu and functions of the web browser software and finally, c) the navigation of the rendering process to create the image displayed on the screen (assembling the

7 Cf. Thierry Bardini: Bootstrapping. Douglas Engelbart, Coevolution, and the Origins of Personal Computing. Stanford 2000.

8 Pat Aufderheide: Interactive Documentaries. Navigation and Design. In: Journal of Film and Video, vol. 67, no. 3-4, Fall/Winter 2015, pp. 69-78, here: p. 72.

9 Ibid., p. 73.

10 Here, 'images' are broadly seen as being programmed, operative and potentially multimodal configurations, cf. Inge Hinterwaldner: Zur Fabrikation operativer Bilder in der Chirurgie. In: Inge Hinterwaldner & Markus Buschhaus (eds.): The Picture's Image. Wissenschaftliche Visualisierung als Komposit. Munich 2006, pp. 206-221; Inge Hinterwaldner: Programmierte Operativität und operative Bildlichkeit. In: Roman Mikuláš, Sibylle Moser & Karin S. Wozonig (eds.): Die Kunst der Systemik. Münster 2013, pp. 77-108.

picture by navigation). That of course also leads to a very specific way of looking at the Internet and at what is being navigated when 'moving' through it. Considering what we have determined until now, isn't what we are doing on the Internet actually navigating *through* and *with* images?

However, navigating the images together is not strictly limited to the Internet. This process of creation is relevant for all kinds of digital images for two reasons.

Methodology and experiment design

What do we gain from reinstating the notion of navigation as a mode, and ultimately a method of inquiry? If we consider the perspective of new materialist informatics inspired by Karen Barad's writing, we may see that the difficulty of documenting networked software principally involves the ontological inseparability of the artwork, the user, and the milieu. In other words, artists' browsers cannot be neatly objectified. Their external effects and embodied affects – what they do to the user – cannot be separated from the user and their interaction with the software. As phenomena, (artists') browsers are complex entanglements of human and non-human agencies. Considering navigation as a method offers us a possibility of making an "agential cut"[11], i.e. a way to distinguish between the "subjects" and "objects" of our inquiry through a set of material navigation practices.

If we acknowledge our own and our interlocutors' interactions with the artwork as a number of agential cuts, we have a better chance of obtaining a less essentialist, that is, less reductive and objectifying account of the artwork in its many facets. We do not try to isolate and disentangle the work from the user and formulate the final, finite, resolved document.

11 Barad, pp. 139–140.

Instead, we arrive at a conjunction of observations, intuitions, feelings, and various documentation approaches. By proposing navigation as a method, we aim not only to compare but to *bring together* multiple embodied perspectives and ways of documenting software.

In the final loop of navigation in our experiment, we asked the contributors to reflect on their own efforts by elaborating on their methodological journey of documentation and drawing things together, thus rendering their specific image of the artistic browser. They elaborate on their methodological journey at the later stage of the experiment. This is the moment when navigation becomes productive as a method for generating insights. It may even enable us to conceptualize novel approaches to documenting software-based artworks and allow for cross-pollination between various fields and disciplines.

A similar approach has already been attempted in the book *10 PRINT*. Here, scholars from code and software studies centered their articles around a single one-line command "10 PRINT CHR$(205.5+RND(1)); : GOTO 10". This minimalistic BASIC program proved extremely inspiring as it became a point of departure and was "treated as a distinct cultural artifact, but it also [served] as a grain of sand from which entire worlds become visible; as a Rosetta Stone that yields important access to the phenomenon of creative computing and the way computer programs exist in culture."[12] The publication seems to promote an experimental approach insofar as all the contributors agreed to accept it as the focus of their attention. However, we could also say, it is a typical multi-authored monograph focused on a unique work and is an established format in the humanities.[13] Adopting an approach opposite to the 'distant reading' or 'distant viewing' often used in digital humanities, their book is said to "operat[e] as if under a cen-

12 Nick Montfort et al.: 10 PRINT CHR$(205.5+RND(1));: GOTO 10. Cambridge/London 2013, p. 5.

trifugal force, spiraling outward from a single line of text to explore seemingly disparate aspects of culture."[14] Ten contributors "chose a process of communal authorship"[15] and thus decided to speak with a single voice while nonetheless offering multiple points of view. This sparked some criticism: "I think that if the authors of 10 PRINT had clearly identified their voices, actively shown disagreement, and argued their points, perhaps regarding the entire method, it would have made a more compelling read instead of the route of anonymous verbosity taken."[16] The criticisms of this book by the programmer Håkan Råberg identified pitfalls that we tried to avoid with our conceptual design.

Our request to the contributors went beyond the analysis of a single browser of our choice and then building up their own interpretative path to or from it. Instead, we aimed to achieve something more binding or authoritative – namely a 'best practice'. The software we selected was *.co.kr*, one of the *%WRONG Browsers* (2000) by the artist duo JODI (alias Joan Heemskerk and Dirk Paesmans).

Our contributors were asked to navigate the web using *.co.kr* and document their journey in any way that they felt suitable. The approaches and media that the participants used were implicitly and explicitly informed by their backgrounds and experience, thus inscribing the difference in the documented interaction. The embodied performance of such navigation acknowledges the researchers themselves as attuned instruments of inquiry. Our aim is not to test and evaluate different audiences, we are not looking to generate user studies. We simply suspect that a modus operandi of 'synchronized research' with a flat hierarchy, comparing the outcomes together and drawing consequences from that for future steps will yield benefits for the research results.[17]

13 For instance on the computer game "Portal": Thomas Hensel, Britta Neitzel & Rolf Nohr (eds.): "The Cake is a Lie". Polyperspektivische Betrachtungen des Computerspiels am Beispiel von Portal. Münster 2015.

14 Montfort et al., p.4.

15 Montfort et al., p.V.

16 Håkan Råberg: Lost in a Maze of Code. In: Computational Culture. A Journal of Software Studies, vol.3, 16.11.2013, http://computationalculture.net/lost-in-a-maze-of-code/ [accessed 31.10.2021].

There is one scientific experimental setup we would like to present to illustrate our specific approach. One of the largest research endeavours of our times in astronomy adopted parallel synchronization procedures.[18] In 2019, four different research groups who were deliberately not in contact with each other were sent on a mission for "blind imaging". They were provided with an identical measurement dataset from radio telescopes located around the world and instructed to derive the theoretical appearance of a black hole from this data. Using their own individual algorithmic techniques, software packages and imaging pipelines, they (re)constructed the data. Finally, they compared and fused their outcomes in order to stabilize one joint message.

In our experiment on documenting one browser, we started from a similar stance. The authors were asked to find an individual solution in isolation and given only the task instruction and the URL where the executable could be downloaded (Fig. 1). To ensure comparability (not for augmenting robustness), we decided to define one case study for all in order to learn how the disciplinary backgrounds and methodological preferences play out in the author's decisions of how to look at this browser, how to document it, how to describe it with which foci and why. Respecting these differences, in our own work, a three-step procedure has proven useful and was also proposed to the potential contributors we approached: a) the actual documentation (including all the screenshots, for instance), b) the polished formulation of the essence of the browser that should be passed on to posterity, and c) after-the-fact self-reflection regarding micro decisions that were taken in order to come to a solution for the challenge posed in b). Most of the divergences were expected in c). Therefore, the first two parts of each contribution needed to be elaborated in order to

17 For this we held a joint authors' workshop on March 25, 2022.

18 EHT Collaboration: First M87 Event Horizon Telescope Results. IV. Imaging the Central Supermassive Black Hole. In:The Astrophysical Journal Letters, vol.875, no.L4, 2019, pp.1-52, DOI: 10.3847/2041-8213/ab0e85; Katherine L. Bouman: Portrait of a Black Hole. Here's how the Event Horizon Telescope Team pieced together a Now-Famous Image. In: spectrum.ieee.org, February 2020, pp.22-29; Paula Muhr: "What We Thought Was Unseeable". Die mediale Konstruktion der ersten authentischen empirischen Bilder eines Schwarzen Lochs. In: Zur Authentizität und Inauthentizität von (medialen) Artefakten, eds. Amrei Bahr & Gerrit Fröhlich. Bielefeld, forthcoming.

form the working basis for the following reflections but are not relevant here. In this issue, we are publishing 'only' the individually preferred approach, the 'best-of-documentation' of the specified browser.

For this endeavour we were able to win the services of a cultural anthropologist and STS scholar (Anne Dippel), a historian of technology (Mirjam Mayer), a game studies scholar (Sonia Fizek), a film director & game designer (GVN908), a trio from business information systems (Barbara Dinter, Sarah Hönigsberg, Henrik Wache), and a cognitive scientist (Maria Hedblom). Extending the experiment by inviting contributors from further domains takes the methodological reflection – that began in our core group – to the next level.

Web browsers impact users, their experience and their Internet

JODI's *.co.kr* browser suggests the user explore a geographically determined subspace of the Internet, namely primarily the (South) Korean websites with the very economically attractive two-letter domain names by autonomously initiating searches with corresponding URLs. The shorter the domain names, the more attractive and expensive they are. This was the case in the mid-1990s and continues to be so today. That means a specific sector of the web – one that turned out to be predestined for financial speculation and thus being strategically laden in terms of economics – is presented on stage as if favourable, while the rest of the Internet has to be typed in by the user themself.

One reason for choosing this browser was the *%WRONG Browser* series' overall importance in the realm of early net art. However, it was also selected because having a lot of theoretical context knowledge is not a significant help when the user is trying to come to terms with the browser. In other words, even if we in our group knew more about the artist duo's oeuvre, this did not catapult us miles ahead of all the contributors we basically asked to jump in at the deep end without prior preparation.

Limitation of the experiment

When designing the experiment, we did not have access to the source code. Thus, there was no possibility to pursue the static code analysis. Accordingly, in our brief, we asked the participants to download and run the executable binary file. For some of the contributors, this added the task of dealing with compatibility issues. We had to consider how the individual software/hardware setup affects the outcome. In addition to that, we suggested to our contributors that they encounter the artwork in a phenomenological manner, lest they have the knowledge and skills necessary to retrieve information from the binary file itself. The aspect of generativity – that would be at least partially visible in the source code – needed to be derived from the captured user experience. In its turn, the user experience may have required the contributor to interact with the browser at the same time as setting up and keeping an extensive visual and technical record of the software's runtime. The description of generativity that may have been inferred from this record would not necessarily be full. There was a risk that some generative aspects would not have been triggered or recorded.

In order for the browser to work, the authors needed to download and install it. The executables for Mac and Windows are freely available online (Fig. 1). We also asked the authors to specify the OS they were working on as the hard- and software constellation might cause differences in the performance of the web browser. In 2021, the newest MacOS versions caused difficulties, and contributors working on Linux needed to emulate another OS. While these differences were welcome, we wanted to keep all other starting conditions as equal as possible for everyone. At the same time, we were aware of being biased to varying degrees due to the point in time at which we could dedicate ourselves to this experiment and our pre-knowledge of the artist duo whose browser we had selected.

Contributions at a glance

Art history: Daniela Hönigsberg first determined what was relevant (behaviours) and second what questions would result in a systematic interrogation of the application. These were mostly related to functionality and interactivity. Her documentation setup was designed to capture a holistic picture of online- and offline activities.

Cognitive science: Maria Hedblom searched for ways to determine the software's purpose and meaning. The plan was to break down the components by cutting their affordances to interaction into functions that then could be depicted metaphorically as image schemata. Due to the specifics of the given software piece, she shifted from interacting to identifying interconnections in terms of activity and from semantics to purpose in terms of focus.

Computer science: Martina Richter's method of systematically approaching the task was to first look at the whole, then break it down into smaller units, analyze them independently and assemble them again. She differentiated between a user perspective and a software specialist perspective, targeting the technical structure of the application by applying decompilation methods.

Design research: Konstantin Mitrokhov invested in a sophisticated setup for the multisensorial capture of the reception situation, leaning towards a video-based ethnographic method. Conceptually, he saw the code performance through a variety of lenses which rendered the situation as partial and open-ended per definition.

Anthropology: Anne Dippel used method of writing a stream of experience and mimicked for the purpose of the experiment an entry into a field diary from a participant perspective.

Game design: GVN908 schematically depicted the processes of gathering and processing documentation while encountering compatibility issues. This visual contribution reflected on the "technological gap", and the frustrations as well as difficulties it posed. In terms of aesthetics or method, the bits and pieces of text mimic the disambiguous quality diagnosed in the browser.

Game studies: Sonia Fizek began with a close reading of the browser performance, then changed to another interpretative 'cruising altitude' (distant reading) that was meant to address the meaning of the piece. She did this by analyzing the displayed HTML code (text).

History of technology: When she began her study, Mirjam Mayer was initially convinced that she could clarify the phenomena by taking notes and reordering her written accounts. She combined vastly disparate data such as collected inventory items or text information on browsers. She switched from distanced observation and the idea of getting rid of obscurity, to immersed interaction and the need for orientation.

Image theory: Inge Hinterwaldner focused on how the elements of the browsers were related to each other and what patterns they formed together. She also relied on further analytical software assisting her criminalistic and forensic approach. After recording the interlacing structures and functions in a relatively unsystematic way, she then set up several series of tests to clarify the unknowns step by step more systematically.

Information systems: Hendrik Wache, Sarah Hönigsberg and Barbara Dinter mapped the findings and identified parameters in a structured table (morphological box). That helped break down the browser performance into smaller elements that were simpler to handle. The table revealed gaps and thus ensured a certain degree of completeness. It also led to the research group inventing labels for everything and could be used as a blueprint for a narrative documentation.

DOI: 10.5282/ubm/epub.93522

Fig. 1, Executables for versions (Mac and Windows) of 11 browsers of the %WRONG Browser series can be downloaded at https://wrongbrowser.jodi.org/.

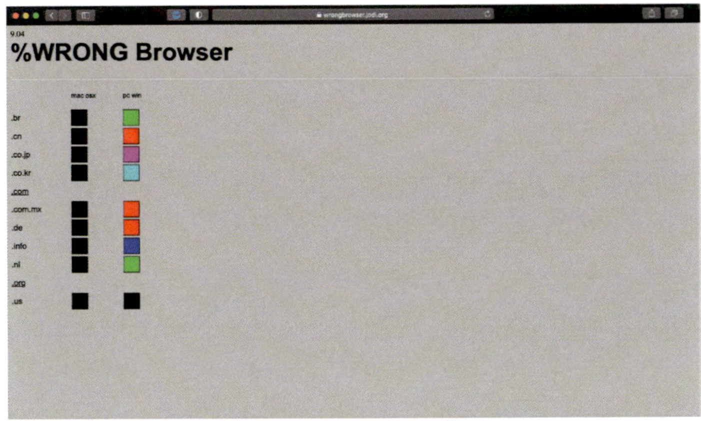

Contributions

Daniela Hönigsberg

Documenting %WRONG Browser .co.kr

There can be no finite procedure that is guaranteed to find all the regularities of an entity.[1]

Conception and preparation

The preparation of the documentation for the *.co.kr* browser of JODI's *%WRONG Browser* series was conducted in an attempt to create a method that would be applicable for all the artistic browsers that are part of our research project. The first step therefore was to contemplate how to capture an artwork that is not only dynamic and responsive to user interaction, but also connected to a complex environment. The central points I determined as relevant for a thorough documentation are as follows:

- The programmed reality of the software, its settings, behaviour and the underlying rules
- The execution of the application, its behaviour and possible user interaction
- The (historical) technical and visual program environment
- The user experience and user behaviour.

The first considerations in this process were of a technical nature: the hardware and software required to run the application, and the tools to create a recording of its audio-visual output. I considered that the optimum way to document the work would be to approximate the original situation in which

1 Murray Gell-Mann: Regularities and Randomness. Evolving Schemata in Science and the Arts. In: John Casti & Anders Karlqvist (eds.): Art and Complexity. Amsterdam 2003, pp. 47-58, here p. 50.

the software was executed. This is what I attempted.[2] The greatest obstacle to this approach is certainly the Internet itself as it has changed considerably in the last twenty years. It represents an extended and highly complex application environment that is virtually impossible to reconstruct – and certainly not in the scope of this documentational experiment.[3] Considering the dynamic nature of the work, the most suitable approach seemed to be to create a video recording of its usage and the moving images presented on the screen. The recording would also include not only the sounds produced by the work itself, but also those resulting from the user's interaction with the computer, such as clicking or typing, as part of the user's experience of the work. It was also necessary to have a recording of me as the user interacting with the program, so a secondary camera was installed in close proximity to my eyes on a baseball cap. Both signal sources, the computer outputs, including system and surrounding sounds and the secondary camera were recorded simultaneously.[4] This low-tech approach (Fig. 1) did not yield the desired outcome because, most of the time, my movement prevented the secondary camera from recording the typing or mouse interaction, and even prevented me from performing natural movements. The secondary video was therefore sub-par and not very helpful in this specific setup. It also created a bigger issue, as predicted, for the informational value of the recorded session. Central aspects, such as the distinction between specific program behaviours that are the result of automated processes and those that are due to interactions with users, were difficult to reconstruct from just the screen capture and thus lost to the documentation and the analysis.

2 I decided to use a computer originating at about the same time as the artwork: MaxData VMX, Modell NB 2000-line Eton Pro 14.1" TFT. The operating system was Windows Millennium (ME) Version 4.90.3000.

3 I contemplated finding a way to limit the bandwidth for example, but there are so many factors to consider, that attempting to revive the internet of 20 years ago would be very difficult and require an elaborate approach. However, this would certainly be an interesting project that would benefit a thorough documentation of historic Internet-based artworks.

4 I used the open broadcast software OBS to record the video on a MacBook Pro with macOS Mojave Version 10.14.6 via a Ba30DEllylelly Mini VGA to HDMI Converter VGA2HDMI Adapter, a Mira Video Capture Box and a Materro Wi-Fi Endoscope Camera Model YPC99-5.

Fig. 1, Technical setup for the recording of the documentation video: MaxData VMX, Model NB 2000-line Eton Pro 14.1" TFT, Windows Millennium (ME) Version 4.90.3000, GL iNet Slate Dual-band Mini VPN Router|Portable Usage for Travel, Home, and Business (GL-AR750S-Ext) connects the XIRCOM RealPort CardBus Ethernet 10/100+ Modem 56 RBEM56G-100 to the wi-fi, Ba30DEllylelly Mini VGA to HDMI Converter VGA2HDMI Adapter, Mira Video Capture Box, MacBook Pro macOS Mojave, Materro Wi-Fi Endoscope Camera Model YPC99-5.

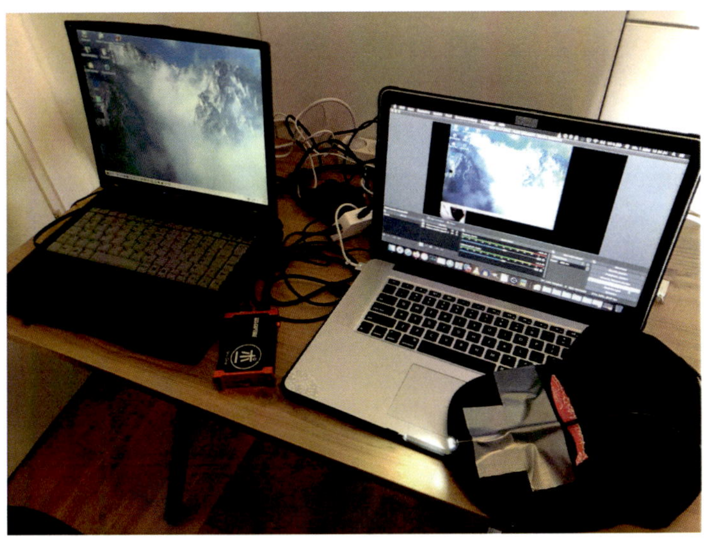

With the technical specifications decided, the next aspects to consider were how to interact with the browser, and what questions or goals to follow during this interaction. The following list of questions was created with the aim of capturing answers in the documentation:

- What does the graphical user interface look like?
- What are the initial settings?
- Does the browser act without user initiative, and what does it do?
- What can the user do?
- What inputs can the user direct?
- What happens after the user directs an input?
- What functions does the graphical user interface offer?
- Is the program's function limited to the browser window?
- Is there an audio output?
- How does the user navigate?
- Are links functional?
- Are there elements or functions familiar from conventional web browsers or browser windows, and which ones?

Initially, the intention was to create a strict sequence of operations for the interaction, so it would be possible to recreate the process and compare the findings. However, as a structured approach was not found, an explorative phase without a strict sequence was included and this became the first part of the documentation.

Exploration phase

The hypothesis used in the exploration phase was that the browser is a graphical user interface (GUI) constructed in a similar way to every other GUI, behaving in a specific way, and containing specific elements that can either be interacted with or not. These specific elements of the GUI have properties that it is possible to discern by looking at and interacting with them. To understand the specificity of the observed GUI, it was consistently compared to a mental aggregational reference

Fig. 2, Aggregational reference model of a GUI with standard graphical control elements: Window, listbox, buttons, scrollbars, menu bar/ toolbar, text box, canvas, check boxes, labels, combo box, toggle switches.

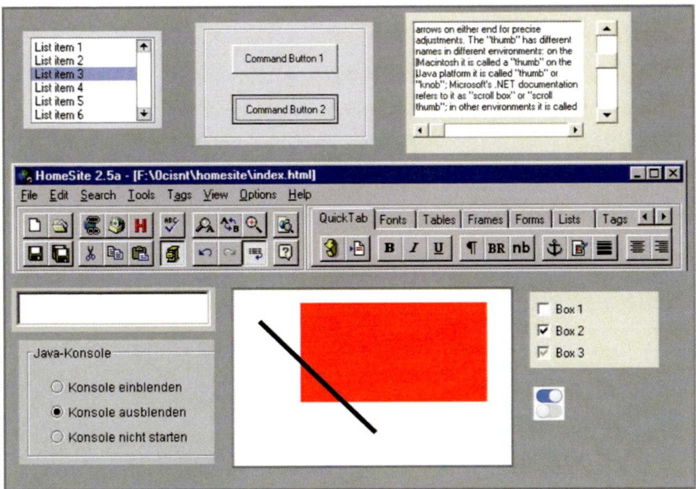

model of a GUI and its potential graphical control elements (Fig. 2). The reasonable assumption that the program is not actually a GUI, is not covered by this approach, which can be problematic because it does not allow for the description of something genuinely new.[5]

The browser was used with the clear goal of finding the aspects of the program that could be identified as discrete elements and functions. Here, the mental reference model was the guide to identifying the different elements, the discrete functions of these elements and their properties by visual inspection over an extended period of time, and by using a multitude of standard behaviours connected to the standard

5 Cf. James P. Crutchfield: What Lies Between Order and Chaos? In: John Casti & Anders Karlqvist (eds.): Art and Complexity. Amsterdam 2003, pp. 31-45, here p. 41.

graphical control elements. The behaviour of the application however, forced me into taking a rather scattered approach. Especially in the beginning, I jumped from one part of the application to the next purely because something caught my attention, or because the element was no longer active in the automated processes of the program, making it impossible to continue the interaction. Thus, the automated behaviour of this specific application was actively preventing me from following a structured approach and I had to adjust my explorative behaviour accordingly.

The first differentiation between the elements was by the presence or absence of any interactive properties. If there was a behaviour visible that was not due to interaction, then it was clear that this was part of the automated program behaviour and dependent on system internal parameters. Next, I determined aspects such as the approximate size of each element in relation to the other elements. The specific relevance of the size is that when this is known, the consequences of two elements overlapping can be discerned, for example. This provides information about their background settings and similar properties. One obstacle is the lack of information regarding the number of elements there are to observe and with which it is possible to interact. Potentially, there could be, for example, elements that are transparent and do not hold any kind of content but are in motion. These elements might perform a variety of activities, but it would be impossible to identify them, and they could still have an influence on other elements. However, this influence would be very difficult to trace. The automated behaviour in many of the *%WRONG Browser* applications is so complex and heavily randomized that it would be necessary to conduct either a very thorough long-term observation of the program, or an investigation of the source code. The perceived complexity of the executed application is a striking example of a problem well described in the theory of complex systems. "As one moves across the spectrum of predictability – from ordered to random behaviour – the "complexity" is maximized in the middle."[6] And without the source code the regularities governing the behaviour are difficult to discern. Nevertheless, with an investment of considerably more time and resources, including an automated interaction, the method proposed here should reveal these irregularities in such a way that is nearly as effective as consulting the source code of the program. However, without accurate time measurement systems – necessary for example to precisely recreate a specific behaviour – it was not possible to consider or approximate these kinds of eventualities. The remaining option was to perform every conceivable common and uncommon interaction in order to reveal the different properties of each element. Thus, I have attempted to click them, mark them, change their position, and stop them behaving in an automated manner. In addition, I deliberately misused elements whose functions were known or supposed, and tested their limits and hidden features to get to their coded identity.

Some aspects could only be documented by repeating the same behaviour and re-starting the application several times. The only time I used this kind of approach was when I wanted to see if the first automatically inserted URL would always be the same when the browser started up, and which one it was. Even though it was possible to gain much information by pursuing different tasks or different theories in multiple sessions, my focus was to stay with the session for as long as it took me to gain the impression of knowing all aspects that are discernible by a continuous interacting and visual inspection. During the whole recording process, I never exited the appli-

6 Cf. James P. Crutchfield: What Lies Between Order and Chaos? In: John Casti & Anders Karlqvist (eds.): Art and Complexity. Amsterdam 2003, pp. 31-45, here p. 41., pp. 36-37.

cation and took no notes. This was necessary to ensure that the application's general behaviour was captured in a pure and representative way, as devoid as possible of any outside factors. Staying with the program for a prolonged time was also crucial because nearly all the elements move constantly and erratically, making it difficult to keep track of them.
The system environment was another aspect that was included in the recorded documentation as part of the experience of the artwork. The interaction with the browser started with opening the application. Observing the program launch is relevant because it allows us to see the application icon and how it is displayed in the operating system's GUI (Fig. 3), as well as the original setting of the application window, the first of the elements to be compared to the mental reference model. The opening of the *.co.kr* browser into full screen is a property of this element and also has the effect of blocking out the entire operating system's GUI. It would be necessary to leave the application to return to anything else. This is a very immersive approach which evokes a reaction from the user that conventional browsers do not pursue. Viewing the setting of the initial application window seems an important aspect for every browser that is a potential candidate for documentation.

What was not included in the recorded documentation was the retrieval of the executable, or information about how to install it on the system, which would have been an equally interesting aspect to include in the documentation.

Textual documentation and analysis

As described, during the interaction, I used and expanded upon a preconceived mental image of the application, filling a mental model of a GUI with information about the identi-

Fig. 3, Application icon displayed in the operating system's GUI (screenshot): Turquoise square labeled CO.KR.

fied elements and the properties they exhibit. However, this constantly evolving image of what the program is and how it behaves was not written down during the exploration phase. The translation into text was performed in the final step of the documentation, using the approx. 40-minute video of the interaction as the reference.

Here, I was able to describe the program behaviour and elements in the structured way that the exploration phase did not allow. It consisted of:

- the description and images of the technical set up for the documentation itself
- (the reference to the video recording)

- a description and screenshots of the initial screen
- the description and screenshots of the overall structure and composition of the graphical interface, which included the description of each identified element and its properties
- a list of accessed websites and comparative screenshots showing the web pages in *%WRONG browser co.kr* and a conventional browser accompanied by notes of observations.

As the video recording was the only additional source of reference apart from my own memory, the previously mentioned shortcomings of the recording method instantly became evident. The recording of typing activity and the use of the mouse cursor would have been extremely valuable for ascertaining which interactions were performed when, and the actual results of these interactions. The video document created during the exploration phase only allowed me to try and track the mouse cursor on the screen itself. Only the behaviour that was visible on the screen recording could be followed, so the description of the program's behaviour and its properties was primarily based on my mental concept of the browser, and the things that I discerned while using it. The video therefore served to confirm these observations and facilitate a more detailed description. It was useful to look at the video to observe aspects that were not on my mind or did not seem of interest during the interaction. If the video recording had included clear footage of typing activity and mouse usage, it may have been just as helpful as the written documentation.

Conclusion

Understanding what could and could not be done, what was happening and what was possible took longer than expected. Most information was gathered by using the browser over a prolonged period of time, finding an understanding of the application, feeling comfortable with what there was to see and interact with, and resolving the confusion or uncertainty that these programs can create in a user.

A next possible step would be a recorded video presentation of the possible behaviours of the program. This would showcase a very goal-oriented user's behaviour, which is probably not to be considered the natural user behaviour one would expect with this kind of application, as it takes time to understand the program and the behaviour of the elements. Such an approach might lead to an accurate documentation of the possibilities for interaction with the browser and a thorough documentation of its elements. However, what would be lacking is the documentation of the behaviour of the user, which seems to be a crucial part of these works as well. That is, to see what users do and what they need to do, to understand what they see and what the program does. On that note, it must be mentioned that any user who does not intend to create a documentation of the *co.kr* browser, and does not attempt to determine its coded regularities, would be likely to show a significantly different behaviour with the application than I did. The inclusion of numerous participants to document different kinds of user behaviour with the program would therefore be another desirable addition to this method of documentation.

DOI: 10.5282/ubm/epub.93523

Fig. 1, Diagrammatic subset of an ontological decomposition of .co.kr's most obvious components, divided into sensory-modalities. Note: the diagram is not exhaustive nor completely ontologically accurate neither in its components nor their transformations.

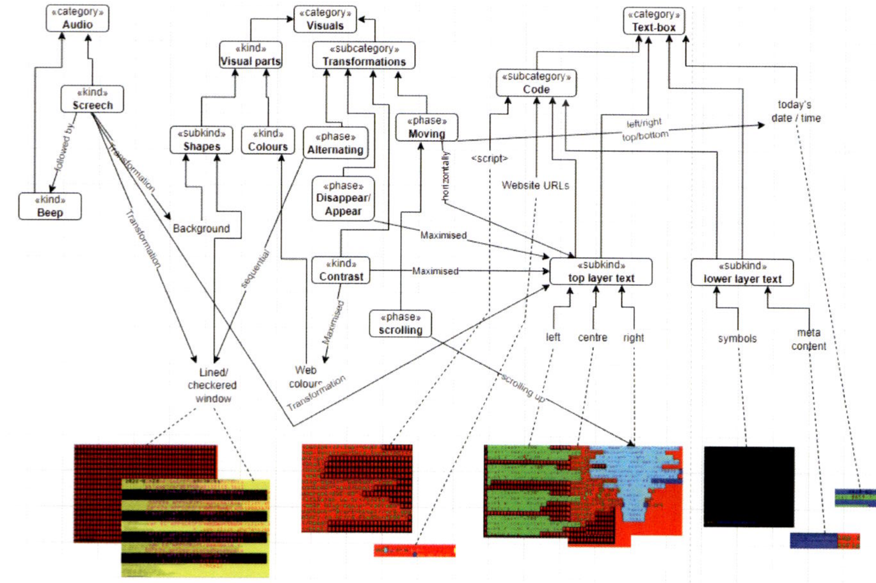

Methodological reflection of the documentalysis of .co.kr from the %WRONG Browser series

1. Introduction, system description and research questions

Invited to participate in the documentation project of *.co.kr* in the *%WRONG Browser* series, I was asked to – to the best of my professional ability – enable the experiencing of a digital art piece in a future when technological advancements and paradigm shifts made it impossible access. Drawing on my scientific background, my usual research method is to formally structure, identify and analyze semantic micro-patterns of concepts[1] and events[2] with the goal of integrating them into formal systems for artificial intelligence. Approaching the task in this way, I performed what for lack of a better word could be called a "documentalysis" (the amalgamation of documentation and analysis) on the art piece. This was a form of interactive, experience-based documentation in which I was trying to separate syntactical parts of the art piece and analyze their semantic content.

During all interactions with the browser, I used an HP laptop running Windows 10 OS and used two additional monitors to write comments about the system and view screenshots of specific components. I ran the program repeatedly during each session to see changes to the initial state and spread my interactions with the systems over several days, which were in turn spread several weeks apart. To structure my findings

1 Maria M. Hedblom, Dagmar Gromann & Oliver Kutz: IN, OUT and through: Formalizing Some Dynamic Aspects of the Image Schema Containment. In: Proceedings of the 33rd Annual ACM Symposium on Applied Computing, New York 2018, pp. 918-925.

2 Maria M. Hedblom et al: Image Schema Combinations and Complex Events. In: KI-Künstliche Intelligenz, no. 33, 2019: pp. 279-291; Maria M. Hedblom et al.: Dynamic Action Selection Using Image Schema-Based Reasoning for Robots. In: Proceedings of the Joint Ontology Workshops, 2021.

and thoughts during the experience, I used Microsoft Word as a text editor on the computer and Google Drive's editor online. For a system overview, I used the open-source software Diagram.net, saved screenshots were cropped and edited in Microsoft Paint and, more often than not, I used the old-school technique of pen and paper to structure my impressions before fitting everything together.

Partially edited in retrospect, and given that research questions are permitted when performing a documentation, the questions that guided my approach to the task were: *How should one interact with the system to find its purpose? And, following the struggle to answer the first question, the more philosophical question: How does one extract meaningful semantics from seemingly randomized syntax?*

2. Designing a "documentalysis" as a journey through scientific theories and methodologies

In my professional experience, almost everything can be decomposed into several more meaningful, or at least more semantically focused, compositions that together construct the whole conceptualization of something. Therefore, in the initial stages of the documentation, I aimed to reverse-engineer the system by decomposing the system's syntax into an ontological hierarchy of its components.

My goal was to find the individual purpose for each of the components based on the interactivity they offered and then separate this interactivity into functionality and/or metaphoric representation. For system functionality, I initially decided on doing a semantic analysis based on affordances[3]; and for metaphor dominant components, I intended to map their semantic

3 James J. Gibson: The Theory of Affordances. In: Robert Shaw & John Bransford (eds.): Perceiving, Acting, and Knowing: Toward an Ecological Psychology. Hillsdale 1977, pp. 67–82, here p. 67.

content to conventional conceptual metaphors.[4] To connect functionality with the (potential) metaphoric representation I planned to do an image-schematic analysis, and thus connect the embodied experiencing of the system to a semantic representation.[5]

For the purposes of reflection, I wrote most of the methodology in this section with the word initially. This is because, while interacting with the *%WRONG Browser,* I realized that I would not be able to perform a very deep analysis of the system following this methodology due to its rather chaotic character. While I was able to immediately identify several different programming components that acted as individuals based on their positioning and their different sensory modalities, I decided to shift my focus from interacting with the system as a whole to identify the interconnectivity between the different components. In doing so, I altered my search for semantics somewhat, by instead looking for the purpose (functional and/or metaphorical relationship) between the system's different components.

3. A U-turn in understanding and three stages of interaction that lead to the documentation

Due to the scientific theory I had selected as a basis, my initial interactions with the browser were not only random in execution but also left me confused in reception. I searched for functionality and interactivity by clicking on different components and attempted to change the interface by writing other URLS into the various text boxes that allowed editing.

Exploring the browser in this way led me to realize that my understanding of the task had been somewhat misguided.

4 Zoltán Kövecses: Conceptual metaphor theory. In: Elena Semino & Zsófia Demjén (eds.): The Routledge Handbook of Metaphor and Language. Abingdon 2017, pp. 13-27.

5 Mark Johnson: The Body in the Mind. The Bodily Basis of Meaning, Imagination, and Reason. Chicago 1987; George Lakoff: Women, Fire, and Dangerous Things. What Categories Reveal about the Mind. Chicago 1987.

I had been under the impression that I was to document an artistic version of an early type of Internet browser, not an art piece within a browser. Not used to these types of tasks, I found it hard to let go of the search for functionality and purpose, and throughout the entire process I found myself searching for interactive functionality regardless.

The second stage of my interactions was more analytical. I reasoned that if I could not find functionality in the system as a whole, I would try to figure out the purposes of particular components.

Consequently, I refocused my original ontological analysis into a preliminary system overview. Instead of looking at the purpose of the collective browser, I tried to identify the ontological character of the individual components and the transformational relationships between them. By combining screenshots with an exceptionally liberal interpretation of how an OntoUML diagram[6] can be constructed, I started drawing an overview of the art piece's sensory modalities and transformational qualities (Fig. 1). Naturally, the static format of a diagrammatic system overview prohibits the complete documentation of a system that is as dynamic in transformation and audio-visuals as this one. As a result, the overview captures only a subset of the system, with emphasis on some of its dominant components and characteristics.

The third stage of my documentalysis was an attempt to reconnect the ongoing documentation to the initially planned research methodology. This stage was based on the findings from performing the system overview and combined with real-time interaction with the system to ensure that the dynamic aspects were followed.

The only interactive functionality I could identify was that some of the text boxes allowed for the input of text and that

6 Giancarlo Guizzardi: Ontological Foundations for Structural Conceptual Models. Enschede 2005.

clicking with the mouse allowed the user to switch between the different text boxes. In terms of affordances, neither of these functionalities allowed for any responsiveness of the system nor displayed any reactivity. Adding text did not, as far as I could detect, change anything in the system. Switching the text box that was currently being edited also did not provide any obvious transformational differences to the system.

Moving from functionality into metaphorical extensions did not make my documentalysis any more successful. While conceptual metaphors might be part of the system's underlying thought and motivation, nothing presented in the system stood out to me as directly conventional. The design choice of always using contrasting colors for text and background, the flickering and transformational consequences of the screeching sound and the scrolling of the text could perhaps be mapped to a metaphorical meaning. However, since the system does not provide any explanations upon which to base such interpretations, any such attempt is likely to be misdirected and would be subject to overfitting.

As I was trying to identify image schemas in the system, I encountered problems similar to those experienced with the previous scientific theories I had used. Image schemas are spatiotemporal patterns that function as conceptual skeletons for higher level concepts and event conceptualizations.[7] This means that many affordances manifest due to the presence of several image-schematic components[8] and conceptual metaphors are often based on an image-schematic skeleton.[9] As neither of these presented themselves in an obvious way in the art piece, extracting the image schemas based on semantic relevance proved difficult.

Instead, I tried to identify some image schemas purely based on their spatiotemporal manifestations. The most prom-

7 Maria M Hedblom: Image Schemas and Concept Invention. Cognitive, Logical, and Linguistic Investigations. Cham 2020.

8 Cf. Antony Galton: The Formalities of Affordance. In: Proceedings of ECAI2010 Workshop on Spatio-Temporal Dynamics, 2010.

9 Cf. George Lakoff: Conceptual Metaphor. In: Cognitive Linguistics. Basic Readings. Dirk Geeraerts (ed.), Berlin 2006, pp.185-239.

inent spatiotemporal patterns in the system are the transformations between the different components. For example, the movement of components on the screen could be described using the image schema PATH (image schemas are written in uppercase to follow convention), the text boxes could be interpreted as CONTAINERS for text and the scrolling of text could be described as an image schema merge[10] of PATH and VERTICALITY (Fig. 2).

However, returning to my research questions and the instructions of the task, it is not clear what mapping such semantic micro-patterns to the system's syntax would offer in terms of identifying the system's purpose. Ultimately, my documentalysis of the system did not answer my initial research questions.

4. Final reflections on the documentalysis

The complexity of the art piece makes it much more difficult to produce any type of documentation that could successfully communicate the full experience to a future user. In this contribution, the compositional components were analyzed in terms of their functionality and their metaphoric extesions in relation to expected semantic content. The dynamic and chaotic nature of the system made it hard to provide a full representation and the scientific theories underlying the methodology used fell somewhat short of the target, and in consequence, failed to answer the research questions.

While not all documentation has answers that can be found, the search for them in this project led me to repeat my interactions with the system several times and I performed my documentalysis in fragments over an extended period. Based

10 Hedblom et al. 2019.

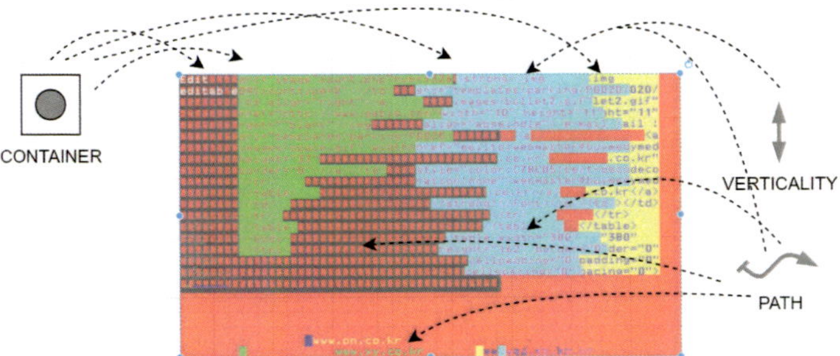

Fig. 2, Example mappings of the image schemas CONTAINER, VERTICALITY AND PATH into components of the art piece (screenshot is set at 50% opacity). The illustration is not exhaustive in terms of either the image schemas or their manifestations.

on this, it is not unlikely that I was inconsistent in parts of the methodology, forgot important considerations and re-emphasized past conclusions regardless of whether new findings presented themselves. Perhaps a more honest documentation would have been done in one sitting, with one interactive analysis and one recording of the system.

Hopefully, the collective documentations in this volume offer the art piece a more comprehensive representation for future preservation than what one contribution alone can accomplish.

DOI: 10.5282/ubm/epub.93524

Fig.1. Structure of the analysis and documentation of JODI's %WRONG Browser.

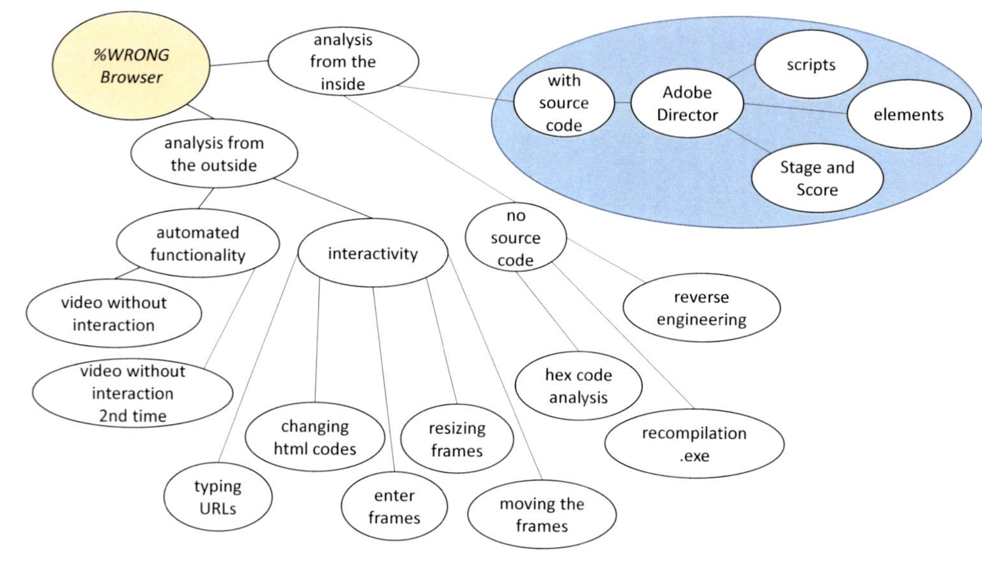

Martina Richter

Descending into detail – a top-down approach to documenting JODI's %WRONG Browser (co.kr.exe)

When I started thinking about how to document the *%WRONG Browser* I wanted to do it in a structured way. As a computer scientist, my general approach when solving a problem is to first look at the whole system, then divide it into smaller, more manageable packages. I follow this procedure in an iterative, recursive and methodical manner. With each division, I continued creating new smaller levels of packages until they had a scope that allowed me to easily access the information I needed. On each level, the packages were examined to either find the next smaller package or retrieve the sought-after information.

With this general approach in mind, my examination of this specific software proceeded in the way I have described. I divided the whole software system into as many parts or elements as I could identify to gain an understanding of how the browser application works.

I also used two theoretical lenses in the method of documenting the browser. The first one – the perspective from the outside of the software – takes into consideration what the user can perceive and experience while using the software. The second – the perspective from inside the software – focuses on finding out as much as possible about how the software is built and how it works in its dynamic processes.

Fig. 1 shows a tree diagram displaying the packages I identified and examined successively and which method and access points of investigation I used. The right side of the diagram shows the from-the-inside approach. The part of that branch that is encapsulated in the blue area contains the part of the analysis which would need the source code and was therefore not included here. That leaves this branch with just limited options. From my disciplinary perspective, it was a challenge to conduct the documentation and retrieve the information about how the browser works without including the source code in the analysis, but I succeeded nonetheless in gathering some relevant information about the inner workings of the program. The artists kindly shared the source code of their work with us later so that an analysis based on the source code is included at the end of this volume.

1 First level of division: Perspectives for looking at the application

The first step in approaching the application was to estimate what system parts could be identified and what perspectives would be most effective in approaching them. For that I established the two lenses I previously mentioned: the outside perspective of the user and the attempt to view the application from the inside by various methods.

1.1 Outside lens - The browser from the user's perspective

Taking the user's perspective, the first question I wanted to answer in my documentation of the *%WRONG Browser* was what the user perceives when using the software. As the user is addressed audio-visually, the media I used to document the perceivable output also had to be audio-visual.

As a second question, I sought to find out what exactly the user is able to do when interacting with the application. In other words: what kind of interactivity does the software offer and what possibilities for interaction result for the user? One option, of course, is not to interact at all and simply watch the application run, observing its behaviour. By addressing these two questions I hoped to capture all possible in- and outputs of the software.

1.2 Inside Lens – The perspective from inside the browser software

The next level of the investigation was to discover and document the technical structure of the application: the view from inside the software. The most important point was to find indications about what programming language was used. This information would yield details about the principal structure of the source code. The structure would differ significantly depending on whether it was a program scripted in an object-oriented language or composed of files created with a multimedia-authoring tool like the Macromedia Director software. It would tell me about certain aspects of the project's programming. In an object-oriented language I would find scripts structured by classes and objects. In the Director files, I would find a stage and a timeline binding the multiple scripts and elements together. The result would be a fundamentally different structure of the application's build.

In this branch of the analysis, I also tried to ascertain the functions and elements of the software and determine how they work together. This also involves finding the necessary steps to do this.

2 Second level of the division - View from the Outside

Having determined the first level of division, I then followed the two resulting branches with suitable methods. First, I focused on the examination of the user's perspective, the view from the outside onto the running application. Here, the perceivable dynamics were the main interest of the investigation. Therefore, I took the role of the user and observed the systems behaviour I was confronted with.

2.1 Observation

To find out if the sequence of what I saw and heard stayed the same with every new execution of the application or whether differences could be observed, I started the application *co.kr.exe* on my PC[1] and first watched the screen output without engaging in any interactions. I took notes of the audio and visual outputs. I started the browser again and did the same for a second time; just observing. The result was that there were distinct differences between the two executions of the application. My conclusion was that an unpredictable element was probably used in the form of a randomizing function, to create the deviating output.

2.2 Interaction

After following that trail, my next aim was to interact with the browser. I started playing around and wanted to find out what possibilities the application offered for interaction. I did that for a while, trying to interact as much and in as many different ways as possible. Then I started to collect the differ-

1 Lenovo MT 20T0 BU Think FM ThinkPad T14s Gen 1 with a Intel(R) Core(TM) i7 - 10510U CPU, running Microsoft Windows 10 Pro 10.0.19042.

ent interaction possibilities, compiling them in a list to then systematically test them in subsequent trails.

The five forms of interactions that I discerned through this initial visual inspection were activities that could be performed with the mouse: clicking, double clicking, dragging and marking. I was also able to interact by entering characters via a keyboard.

2.3 Documentation of the interaction and documentation tools

As I compiled my collection, the next step was to work out how to document the identified possibilities of interaction.

The aim was to record the visual screen output as well as the sound. Obviously, the appropriate way to address this was to take videos of the screen. Because screenshots cannot show timing, movements or sounds, I discarded that idea immediately. Using the list of opportunities of interactivity, I systematically created separate videos of about 2–3 minutes for each element of the list, showing only the one targeted interaction.

The challenge was to find a suitable PC application that could record the whole screen as well as the sound output and that could be started and stopped by keyboard commands – necessary to prevent the process of switching from the record application to the *%WRONG Browser* from becoming part of the recording. This was important because it allowed me to create clean and discrete videos of the specific interaction behaviours without any distracting activities that were unconnected to the targeted interactions. Unexpectedly, it was not an easy task. It took a long time to find and try different applications. After several trials, I found that OBS Studio fulfilled all my above-mentioned requirements.

The result of this step was two videos without interaction and one for each of the five interactions, a total of seven videos, each several minutes long.

3 Second level of division- View from the Inside

As described above, the second part was to look at the application by applying an inside-lens and to document these findings as well. My aim was to go into the software and divide it into as many parts as possible on a technical level. I wanted to find out how the software was developed and in which programming language. I also wanted to extract the code, to examine the techniques, to identify the components used on the programming level and to see what else I could find just by having the application running on my computer.

3.1 Working without the source code

Normally when software is analyzed on the technical level to determine its functionality, its source code is available to be studied. The source code can be divided into its elements and functions which allows me to analyze what exactly happens while I am running the application.

In this case, I had to find ways to gain equivalent information from the executable application. I followed the idea of reverse engineering, that means the approach of drawing as much as possible from the binary file in order to analyze the system parts and how they work together. That can be done on different levels: on the binary file itself, on a disassembled/ assembler level, that is on a machine language level, and finally on a decompiled level, which means creating a source code in a high-level programming language out of the binary file that is not the originally programmed one but which performs in the same way.

The different approaches I adopted and describe below were not selected or applied in a strictly goal oriented manner but were rather forensic in nature. I tried a variety of methods in order to gain as much information as possible and use this to develop a better understanding of the application's source code and how it is structured.

3.2 Binary file

Applications are usually programmed in a high-level computer language. These are computer languages that are easy for humans to read and write, e.g. C, Perl, Java, or Python. For the computer to read or understand these languages, the code has to be translated into binary code. The result of this translation is the executable program. However, in this form, the code is more or less impossible for humans to read.

The executable binary file of the application analyzed here, is downloadable as a zipped file cokr.zip here: http://wrongbrowser.jodi.org/. I started by extracting it to co.kr.exe and examining the binary file.

3.2.1 File properties

When looking into the file properties of the executable by a right mouse click, I found some general information about the application (Fig. 2). Looking at the tab "Allgemein" (General) one can see the date and time of the compilation and that it is a Macromedia Projector file. Going to the tab "Details" yields additional information about the Macromedia Director Version.

This information proved useful because knowing the development environment of an executable allows me to find decompilation methods that are particular to the specific version of the environment. The fact that it was a Macromedia Projector file led me to the next step, which was to look for a method or an application to extract more information from the source code by decompilation.

Fig.2, .exe-file property menu window.

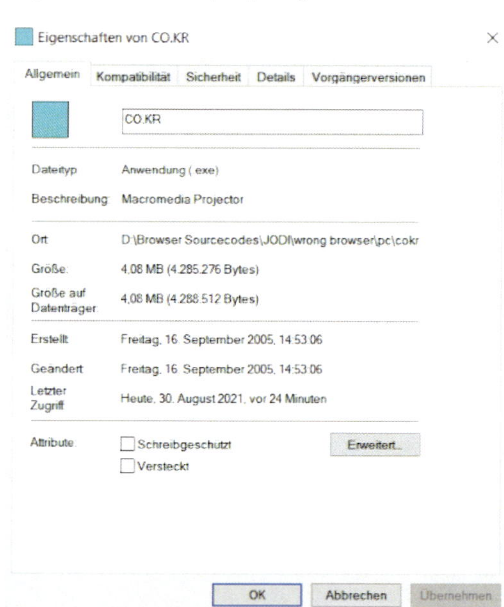

3.2.2 Disassembling with a Hex Code Viewer

With the application PE Explorer it was possible to depict the binary co.kr.exe file as a hex coded file. The hex code depiction of a binary file always shows 4 bits together as a hexadecimal number. This display is slightly more readable than a mere series of '0' and '1'.

I used some tools of the PE Explorer to collect additional information and "read" in the binary file. Looking through the information, I was able to identify the operating system on which the source code was compiled, the date and time of compilation and the processing unit.

I also learned more about the software dependencies, meaning what external software libraries were used to compile the source code. I also was able to obtain and save a list of used strings.

The PE Explorer software is able to disassemble the hexadecimal file. This makes it possible to access an assembler software level. Assembler is a machine-near software or language level between high-level language and binary code. The disadvantage of this code level is that no understandably structured source code is being generated. The variables are not discernible and the result is extremely long (in this case 24,988 lines of code). The created code differs so much from the original source code, and is on such a machine-near level, that it does not lead to a significantly better understanding of the code. Or at least it would have taken a very long time to gain any useful information. Therefore, the next step was to try and find a way to further decompile the code to reach a high-level language.

It was possible to gather some information by looking at the hexadecimal coded file and even more when this code was disassembled, but in the end it did not help me to understand how the software works or to determine the structure of the source code.

3.2.3 Decompiling

I embarked on a longer period of Internet research: which applications could help me to obtain more information about the Macromedia Director source code (which is composed of the scripts, elements, score etc.) or even get the source code by decompiling the executable application? I read a lot in blogs and Internet forums, trying to gain a better understanding of what a Projector file is and my chances of success. The results of my research were rather disappointing. I realized that the chances of gaining any insights were very limited and my goal of getting the source code was clearly out of reach using these methods.

My research also revealed the general limitations of decompilation: the decompiled executable application provides a source code that corresponds to the executable, but it will never be the original source code. The reason for that is that programming is never unambiguous as it is possible to reach the same goal, to produce the same effect in the executed program behaviour with completely different source codes. As mentioned before, original variable names and also comments will be missing in the created code because they can not be reconstructed from the binary code and therefore get replaced by random characters or numbers. This detracts immensely from its readability and the chances of understanding its structure. Disregarding these discouraging prospects, I tried two ways of decompiling the binary code of the project.

3.2.3.1 From .exe to source code

My Internet research did not reveal any application that would decompile Projector files, the executables created with Director. Although the language used in Director is Lingo, I turned to an application that usually is used for C++-.exe. My aim was to determine what the result looks like in principle and whether it was worth putting any more energy into it. As previously described, the executable does not offer any kind of information about the high-level language used to write it. Consequently, the result is something that presumes the program was written in C++ and creates a code that could theoretically be the source of the executable in that language.

This procedure produced a result but it was unreadable (Fig. 3). There are, of course, no original variable names, there is no understandable structure, no modules, objects or classes. So all the features or properties that make a code readable and understandable for humans, are not part of the decompiled code.

3.2.3.2 From .exe to Shockwave flash

During my research I found an entry in a Macromedia forum with someone asking for a way to decompile a Shockwave Flash file.[2] This post and numerous other search results pointed to a close relationship between Projector files and Shockwave Flash files – because Lingo is the main language used for Adobe Shockwave Flash, making it potentially possible to use similar tools on both. I had already gained some experience with decompiling Shockwave Flash files during the analysis of another artistic project. Using the same tools on this executable, I hoped to create a Shockwave Flash file, from

2 Anonymous: Help decompiling SWF! In: stackoverflow.com, 11.11.2010, https://stackoverflow.com/questions/4150912/help-decompiling-swf [accessed 27.8.2021].

which I could extract Director elements like scripts, images, sounds, timing etc. I looked at several applications, but only some of them allowed the executable to be used as the source for the decompilation. In the end I tried two different applications but the results were as disappointing as with the previous trials. I was only able to extract shredded information, like a vector shape (*.nl*) (Fig. 4) and the frame of a graphical element as well as a white dot (*.com*) for other browsers of the *%WRONG* Browser series I used to see if, in theory, results could be achieved with this tool. But for the *.co.kr* browser nothing at all could be found.

4 Conclusion

The attempt to decompile the executable file concluded my documentation of the *.co.kr* browser. Where the outside-lens on the second level of division provided some information regarding the perceivable elements and the user's options for interacting with them, the underlying structures that were to be explored with the inside-lens remained mostly untouched and therefore could not be documented without the inclusion of the source code. The insights gained when the source code was used in an analysis will be included in a separate text in this volume.

DOI: 10.5282/ubm/epub.93525

Fig. 3, Screenshot of the disassembler showing part of the assembler code of the .co.kr.exe.

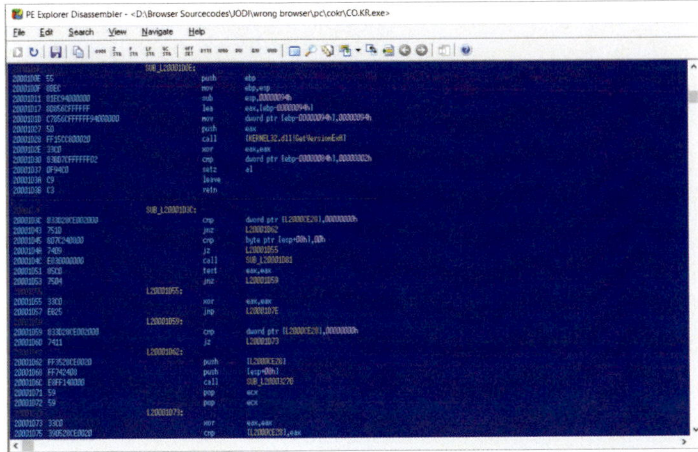

Fig. 4, Screenshot of the result of decompiling the .nl %WRONG Browser.

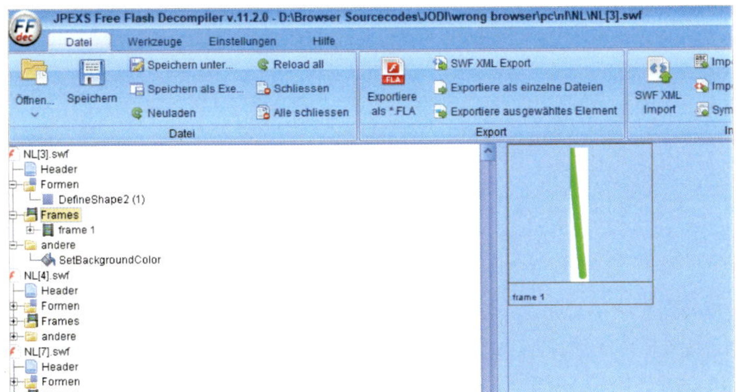

Fig. 1, This conceptual scheme partially renders the relations and traces that arise from an artist browser's runtime. Some of these are recorded (marked in magenta), constituting the relational document that captures fragmentary impressions of what it is like to use the software.

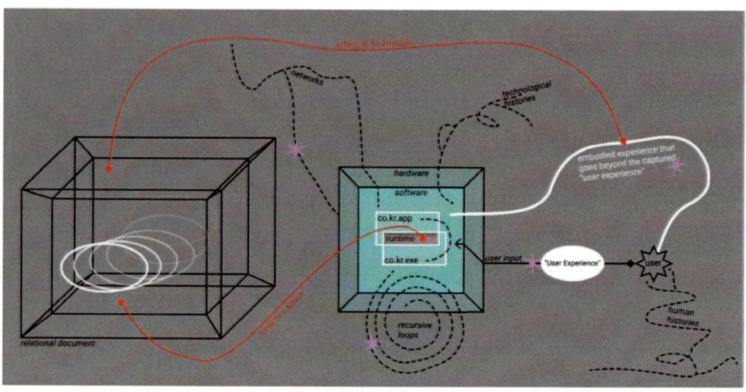

Fig. 2, The distribution of color on a circular scale within a frame from the screen recording of JODI's .co.kr that was running without user input, as displayed by the color monitoring Vectorscope tool found in Final Cut Pro X.

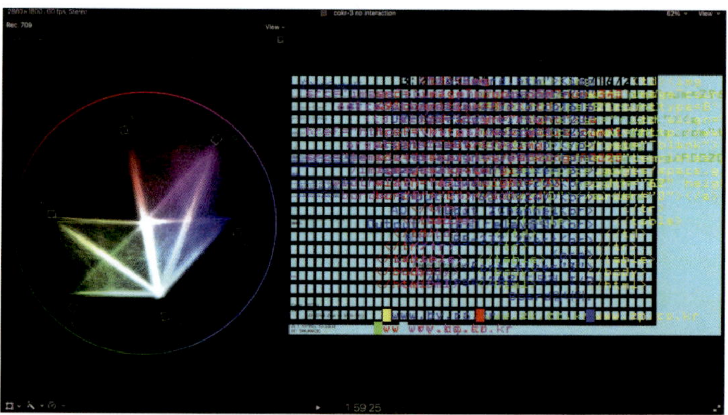

Relational Documents: Capturing Inter-activity of %WRONG Browser

I had a clear goal in mind when I first approached the task of documenting artists' browsers. In response to numerous approaches in new media & software studies, I planned to capture what goes on in front of and behind the computer screen. In computer science, the user is often seen through their interaction with the software. User equals user input. This instrumental, abstract view of the user is supposed to render all users as equal and without bias, but it leaves out the embodied, material, situated nature of each and every interaction. Inspired by Lisa Blackman's notion of haunted data, I think about the studied browsers as code that bears traces of "human and technological histories that are displaced, occluded, erased, disqualified, forgotten".[1] The work – seen as a technical object, that is, an executable binary file – unfolds in time through and by means of the user's interaction with it. In other words, software is performative and its documentation must attend to its affective and material dimensions in order to counteract the instrumental reduction of the user (Fig. 1). For this purpose, I have tended towards an approach based on sensory ethnography: capturing multiple audio and visual perspectives pertaining to the code's execution, studying the materials separately, and bringing them together in a video collage. A precedent to this technique is the Dullaart-Sakrowski method of documenting web-based art that aims to "capture the reception of net art in an environment in which it was originally perceived."[2]

1 Lisa Blackman: Haunted Data. Affect, Transmedia, Weird Science. London 2019, p.xiii.

My initial desire was to capture the relationality of the encounter between the user (me, under current conditions), the technical object(s) of the artwork, the host hardware/software, and the networks of which *.co.kr* is a part. Whenever it was possible, I recorded the work's screen output, audio, and logs of the work's runtime; the external perspective that approximated what I was seeing; and the ambient sound of me interacting with the piece. This, together with my embodied user experience, constituted the core document that I would be expanding on in the iterative process of diffractive (re-)reading, cycling between optics that would help me delve into the work's specificity. It is important to acknowledge, however, that such a process brings the artwork in touch with an embodied and enacted ethico-onto-epistem-ology, thus always co-constituting the work's documentation and the artwork itself. The "raw", unprepared, uncut video documentation of my (non-) interaction with the software is an episteme that I can build upon iteratively while acknowledging that process is transforming my understanding of what the work does and how.

In my conceptual framework, the account of the code's performance is relational, situated, necessarily incomplete and self-reflexive. There is no end to this process. I distinguish between five diffractive lenses – or, alluding to Blackman again, movements – that circumscribe research subjects and would aid my embodied exploration and diffractive reading. Affective (user experience); historical (exhibition, reception, long life of the work); socio-political (funding and institutional contexts); ethical (labour and software/hardware dependencies); technical (critical reading of the source code).

My iterative process was initially based on a number of premises that, as I quickly found out, do not evenly apply to all the works that fall within the scope of our research. The

2 Cf. Kimberley Spreeuwenberg: Documenting Internet-based Art. The Dullaart-Sakrowski Method. In: Culture Vortex, 2012, http://aaaan.net/documenting-internet-based-art-the-dullaart-sakrowski-method/ [accessed 15.6.2022].

premises themselves are rooted in the contemporary software environment that I am familiar with from the last decade of networked software and accelerated cycles of development and dissemination. A perfect candidate for documentation would be free/libre open-source software that is either web-based or runs on one of the browser platforms such as Chrome or Firefox; written in an interpreted language such as JavaScript and therefore by design providing access to the source code; performing consistently across supported platforms; either altering or augmenting the navigation instead of disrupting it. Due to their architecture, these works' interactivity and networked performance could be captured (at least on the user client's side) in minute detail by widely available instruments such as Chrome DevTools.

JODI's *.co.kr* breaks with nearly all of the above criteria. The work is distributed as a 32-bit executable binary file that does not run on my work computer with macOS 11.4. The file worked on the old personal laptop, to which I no longer have access as of July 2021. The standalone software does not reveal its inner structure even when analyzed with specialized software (as attempted by my colleague Martina Richter). There is no artist statement disseminated via the work's website or with the executable file itself. There is no access to the source code.[3] The experience of using the software felt almost hostile as *.co.kr* does not allow for the sustained interaction I was expecting from the software, often disrupting whatever I was trying to do and thus discarding the familiar user experience. Video documentation revealed my impatience and disorientation when interacting with the browser. JODI's browser disrupts the user's expectation of a smooth, continuous experience while not providing access to the technical and ethical aspects of the work that are legible in, e.g. free/libre open-

3 Eventually the artists granted us access but the outcome is not reflected in this text.

source software. It is a metaphorical grey box, neither transparent in its workings nor fully obscuring its networks.

After spending two hours with the work I decided to pause for a week. The work frequently crashed and its vivid, rapidly flashing colors made it difficult for me to engage with it for more than a few minutes at a time. It was not clear if it was my interaction causing the crashes or the work was generally unstable on my computer. At that moment, I acknowledged to myself that I had not participated in prior interviews conducted by our team with JODI, had not read the interview transcripts, nor had any prior encounters with their work outside the scope of this research project. My expectations towards the work were primed by a single video referenced by my colleague Daniela Hönigsberg.[4] It was only due to that video (of which I do not know the precise origin) that I knew that *.co.kr* behaved differently on my hardware/software as it remained silent during the runtime. I confirmed my observation with the team based on their own accounts and video documentation of *%WRONG Browser* runtime on contemporary and legacy versions of Windows.

Once it became clear that there is an element of functional contingency to the work, I had to rethink my method. I had perceived the crashes and digressions of the user experience due to varying hardware and software as failures of the work's generativity. The work's instability had already disrupted my attempts to use it as a browser to such an extent that I had given up hope of capturing any interaction. I realized that I would have to alter my core approach significantly: my intended documentation setup had not yielded much material, while the lack of access to the source code had eradicated any possibility of a close and critical reading. In response, I decided neither to interact with the artwork nor capture the

4 Cf. Anonymous: Wrong Browser. Video, colour, sound, 10 min, 3.1.2020, https://www.youtube.com/watch?v=WaP6-xA77rY [accessed 15.6.2022].

embodied material perspective and instead focus on the contingencies, thus adding the lens of (non-)functionality failure to my diffractive toolkit.

Intuitively, I found new documentation strategies that de-emphasize the (partially denied) phenomenological experience of the browser: looking for interaction opportunities; searching for the browser's functional limits; deducing the source of runtime crashes; comparative engagement with my own and others' documentation in order to find out which aspects of the work are hardware-dependent; not engaging with the work at all, not even observing, and leaving it to run as long as possible. These micro-strategies minimize and instrumentalize interaction with the software, focusing instead on finding out new facts by comparison and disjunction. In other words, the relationality of the embodied encounter with the software gave way to the relationality of the situated software runtime in my documentation process.

Another set of newly emerged strategies counteracted the intensity and speed of the runtime. These relied on high fidelity video capture of the work's runtime and particular watching strategies that disengaged me from the generative temporality of the work in lieu of a pace I could choose myself. These ways of watching proved useful: starting with the originally captured footage; skimming back and forth; watching the footage frame-by-frame while focusing on specific graphic elements and motion patterns; using image analysis tools in video editing software; watching at 4x/8x/16x speed in order to re-cognize the patterns that may not be perceivable during the runtime. These strategies allowed me to break away from the disorienting cinematic continuity of the browser and resist the sensory overload.

It is worth elaborating on my use of Vectorscope tool (Fig. 2) found in Final Cut Pro non-linear editing software (FCP further in the text). I use FCP for independent work outside the scope of this research project, which currently involves production, editing, and post-production of short films. Vectorscope is one of the instruments built into FCP, designed and typically used for color correction of digital video footage. The tool visually represents the distribution of color in one frame, thus allowing to match the palettes of different scenes, ensure the skin tone is neutral, the hues of highlights and shadows are consistent, and so forth. I repurposed Vectorscope for a frame-by-frame reading of *%WRONG Browser*'s video documentation that is often fast-paced and overstimulating when played back. For the purpose of this experiment, I skipped over the editing part of the workflow, instead importing original videos and focussing on their visual analysis. Editing is essential to making a documentary film, yet I was not concerned with having a cut that engages the viewer's attention. Moreover, that would go against the purpose of our documentation experiment. This way of working with FCP is the opposite of making a film, as keeping the attention of the audience is not a concern when documenting an artwork for posterity.

After identifying strategies for dealing with the browser's instability, I read through the team's interview with the artist duo in the hope of finding new optics for reading the user experience of *.co.kr*. One of the references that came up was teletext. A quick query on the web revealed that some of JODI's browsers share many graphic elements with the teletext systems of the 1980s. Saturated colors, a high contrast palette, a pixelated typeface often set very large, no images. I have no first-hand experience of teletext as it was not in use where I grew up in the 1990s. Despite that, when I looked at the works alongside my very limited knowledge of teletext, it significantly altered the way I perceived them. My experience with the internet since the early 2000s and the phenomenological transparency of contemporary browsers were so deeply ingrained in my thinking that I did not consider a different frame of reference for the work.

Neither my documentation of *.co.kr* nor my structured description of the documentation methodology are complete. During my negotiation of the methodology I abandoned some parts of it – if only for this particular series – but it nevertheless proved to be productive. The desire that broadly guides my documentation process is to find out what the work does based on my own experience and then to situate the work in a larger socio-cultural context. *%WRONG Browser* enacted a certain degree of hostility towards me as a user and that is (part of) what the work is (presumably) programmed to do, but my documentary intentions shifted throughout the process, too. My toolkit for diffractive reading still stands, albeit in an expanded form. However, I could reformulate the task of documentation as follows: capture and understand why the work does what it does while moving between the work's registers of doing something on the internet to doing something on my computer to doing something to me, the user.

DOI: 10.5282/ubm/epub.93526

Domain erwerben

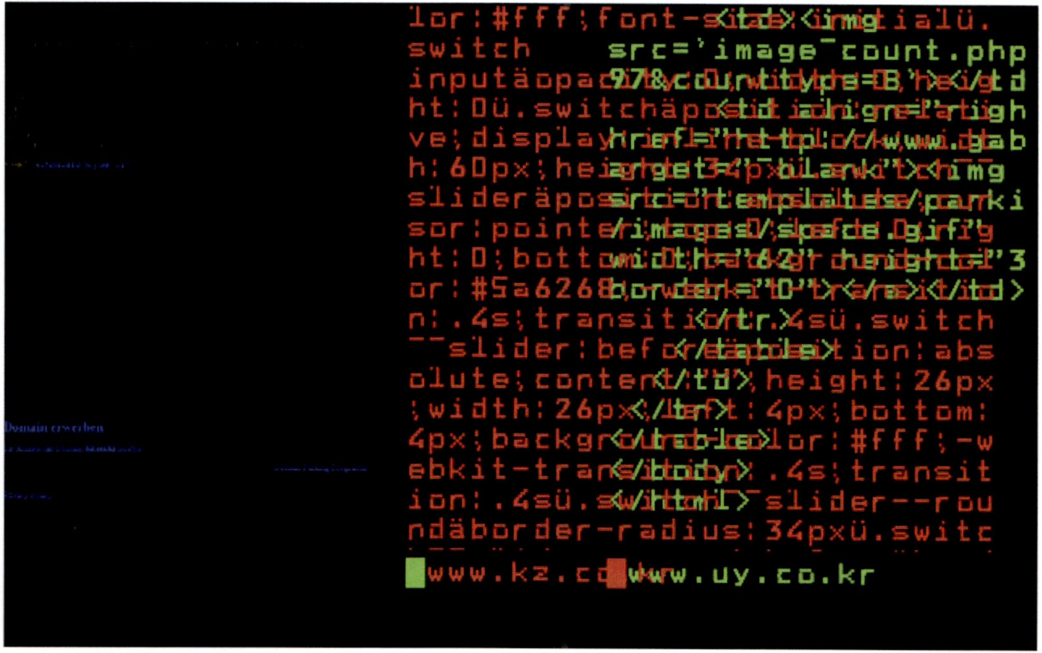

```
lor:#fff;font-s[...]ialü.
switch
inputäopac[...]
ht:0ü.switchäpo[...]
ve;display[...]
h:60px;hei[...]
slideräpo[...]
sor:pointe[...]
ht:0;bott[...]
or:#5a6268[...]
n:.4s;transiti[...]4sü.switch
--slider:bef[...]tion:abs
olute;conten[...]height:26px
;width:26px[...]t:4px;bottom:
4px;backgr[...]lor:#fff;-w
ebkit-tran[...].4s;transit
ion:.4sü.s[...]slider--rou
ndäborder-radius:34pxü.switc
www.kz.co
```

```
<td><img
src='image_count.php
97&count_type=3'></td
<td align="righ
href="http://www.gab
arget="_blank"><img
src="templates/parki
/images/spacer.gif"
width="62" height="3
border="0"></a></td>
</tr>
</table>
</td>
</tr>
</table>
</body>
</html>
www.uy.co.kr
```

anne dippel

a piece of flash

ethnographic observation log

neon colors, primary colors, primate visions. flicker images, black grids, red background, primary colors, primate visions, flicker images, eyes sore, primate visions, headaches, letter arches, primate visions, neon colors. flicker images, grids, grids, grids, matrix, lines falling
down
falling lines, falling codes
code as art, code as technology
browser art, brwsr rt
creative work of art, crtv wrk f rt
technology of creation – creations of technology: enchantment, magic encoded & primate visions of animism.
eye candy, poppy colors, primate visions, who said so – donna haraway did, primary colors, programming language, superimposed signs, reading line: “high school”, time flies,
www.sb.co.kr www.xz.co.kr.

<td>
</tr>
</tabl>
</body>
</html>

column of numbers, column of signs, column of numbers and letters, falling lines, enchantment of art, magic of falling letters, *buchstaben*, beech bars, f

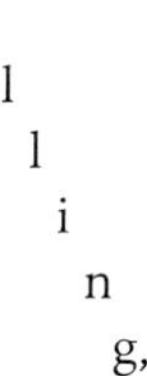

glamor, glamorous graphics, oracles of technology, art of technology, emanations of self-similarity. “whereas for warburg, the logic of the image is the pathos (i.e. the emotional pull), for boas and subsequent theoreticians in anthropology, the survival of the image rests not in its relation to pathos, but in its own self-similarity. the nature of self-similarity is one wherein the form is an isomorphic configuration of an idea of relation. this idea, in being externalized – or concretized – in an object, becomes an image, manifesting the patterns that are analogical to the social world.”[1] anthropology, the art of superimposing the social and the technological, the entanglement of objects and humans. columns of numbers and letters, falling lines, falling, falling, green – blue – red – magenta – black grids flickering

– coal, transparent, discrete, time passing, time critical, time, gone, time, gone, browser gone, flash ephemeral, browser ephemeral, me, ephemeral, art, passing. </soft></body></html>, domain, domain, domain.

code evolution, code superimposition, latin letters, korean letters, 한글 han’gŭl, discrete manifestations of sound, semiotics, sign and difference, </soft></body></html> what domain? what body, what? what metaname descriptions keywords, what? meaning? interpretation gone. ricketflicketitricketishriggle, tripple, eyes ripping out of caves, can’t stare, can’t stand, flickering images, closing eyes, internet fictions,

1 susanne küchler & timothy carroll: a return to object. in: alfred gell (ed.): art and social theory. new york 2021, p. 2.

futures lost.
no hermeneutics possible.
neon colors, primary colors, primate visions. “what the hell is going on here?”, who said so – people say, clifford geertz did, but i never found the quote when i tried to look it up. word of mouth, alas, becomes truth if the right authority figure says so. flicker images, black and blue strips, black background, memories of missed updates, memories of missing fonts, memories of text editors, memories of web 1.0. primary colors, primate visions, flicker images, eye sore, primate visions[2], headache, primate visions, neon colors, headache spanning body and mind. flicker images, grids, grids, grids, matrix, lines falling out of screen, out of shot, out of interface, losing face, falling colors, falling codes, code as art, technology as enchantment, who said so, alfred gell did[3], browser art, brwsr rt, creative work of art, crtv wrk f rt, technology of creation, creations of technology, repetitions, repetitions, circles, circuits, governing enchantment, primate visions of animism, eye candy, poppy colors, primate visions, primary colors, programming language, superimposed signs, reading lines “high school”, time flies, no time for hermes, www.sb.co.kr www.xz.co.kr, kybernos is steering, www.sb.co.kr www.xz.co.kr, delete repeat, enter

<td>
</tr>
</tabl>
</body>
</html>

end of hermeneutics, “anti-hermeneutical reflexes”, who said so? memories of student disputes with paul feigelfeld return, code, language, ghost, machine, primate visions, affect art, ricketflicketitricketishriggle, tripple. <beauty lies in the eyes of the programmer>. <animation lies in the eyes of the beholder>,

2 donna haraway: gender race and nature in the world of modern science. new york 1990.

3 alfred gell: the technology of enchantment and the enchantment of technology. in: jeremy coote & anthony shelton (eds): anthropology, art and aesthetics. oxford 1992, pp. 40-63.

Fig. 2 and 3, Handwritten sketches by the author.

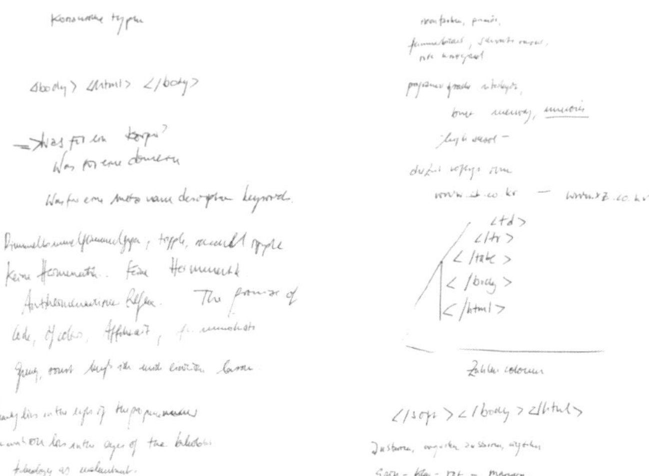

<animism is embedded in the code based on hardware>. software, softer, softest ware, primate visions, switching off. end of stream of consciousness, "stream of experiences", who said so, i did[4], (<yes, that's me a past me, gone>), end of stream of impressions, close this field diary, close my fingers, close the keyboard; end of social relations emanating from code, end of social relations embedded in code, promises, promises, switch off all machines, who said so? friedrich kittler did allegedly, at last, this is what tania hron, alma kittler and susanne holl said, who were there, when he left this world. switch off this old apple 13 inch, mid 2013, processor 1.3 ghz intel core i5, memory 4gb 1600 mhz ddr3 start up disk macintosh hd graphics intel hd graphics 5000 1563 mb, serial number c02krmpuf5v8, OS X yosemite, system report, me no serial number, cokr did not quit unexpectedly, consciously switch off this piece of flash. done.

4 anne dippel: der erlebnisstrom. ein werkzeug ethnographischen schreibens. in: berliner blätter, no. 1, 2015, pp. 72-83.

this document is a threefold ethnographic mimicry. first, it mimics the programmed interface and the personal experience of a human being when engaging with jodi's *%WRONG browser*. since ethnographers use their own senses, mind and body as a means to gather, process and analyze data, the above text describes the emotional and affectual reactions of the user – including memories and immediate experience. second, it mimics a human way of relating and connecting through mirroring and mimicking the other's point of view. it is thus a meta-commentary on the specific anthropological condition to animate whatever is moving, especially when it comes to engaging with digital media technologies. and third, it mimics the private nature of a field diary, in which anthropologists memorize and reflect on empirical experiences collected during their field work. it was the technology itself that allowed me to associate, as a form of enchantment quite similar to the experience of going into a museum and reflecting, reacting, being exposed to art works. the notification of the beginning and end of the program was another form of mimicking coded pathways, not typical for stream of experience, but typical for a stream of experience that reflects this specific browser art software. while watching the program, associations come to mind. the notes of the field diary are notes of the now, but in the aftermath, due to hermeneutical reflections, new thoughts emerge, that bind the imagery into narratives, memories and existing concepts. one could think about popular visualizations of online worlds and falling words such as those famously portrayed in the movie *matrix* (1999, wachowski sisters), but the program was too strong in its visual impressions and its neon colors typical for the era in which it was developed. i tried to focus on this singular phenomenon and use it as a figurative gateway for accessing current discourses on how to read digitality and its transformations. there is no story in this program, no narrative that would help to make and give sense. watching it unfold, the inner worlds of thought could empty themselves – the failed attempt to lay a hermeneutical circle on, developing theoretical contexts and binding it by a narrative of experience allows the user to circumvent the void, the utmost anxiety that comes with the meaningless flow of images, and falling, flowing characters and numbers.

the associative play with sound and poetry within the text, the mixing of memory, quotations and fragments of meaning that dis-rupt the mere documentation, are designed as a meta-commentary on how alien digital code seems to human's way of making sense of things. the hopes encoded in artistic visions such as jodi's *%WRONG browser* mark a historical moment in time, when hermeneutic approaches failed to understand what is actually going on in software. at the same time hermeneutics today has become more important than ever, since the infrastructure of technology is leading to new narratives, transforming communities and values. while the technological enchantment of early programming left the impression that hermeneutics would become useless, we see the opposite happening these days, precisely because of the visual and non-narrative structure of most software permeating everyday life. the artistic take aims to illustrate that as much as ethnographic description is rope dancing between poetry and prose, between observation and imagination, it is always the source of new understandings by engaging empirically with the world and reflecting reality. i write field diaries either by hand or using a text editor. since i am a very fast typer (depending on the text ca. 400–600 characters per minute) i can write on my computer as fast as i can speak, or sometimes even think. this makes me cautious. i prefer writing by hand because it encourages me to formulate my thoughts more concisely and form teleological sentences (the point at the end of the sentence is integrated in the first word written when formulating a thought). i watched the browser on an old computer and typed directly into the text editor. i watched it twice. the first time, i made some notes by hand. they were first sketches, first ideas. and unfolded into coherent thoughts when writing the stream of experience, filling impressions with memories, quotations and sense.

last but not least, citation of art history and anthropology as two distinct traditions for interpreting the relationship between art and technology is encoded as a promise and a riddle that leads like an ariadne's thread back into the world of hermeneutical understanding, where any piece of art, any browser, any code is simultaneously the expression of social relations and the human capacity to build any kind of togetherness and find meaning where meaning is absent without participation and participant observer. my documentation shares how I am failing to make sense and establish sense at the same time when being exposed to certain realms of digitality for the first time, such as those shown in this browser art.

DOI: 10.5282/ubm/epub.93527

GVN908

The Crack

[The contribution is reproduced on pages 72–77]

DOI: 10.5282/ubm/epub.93528

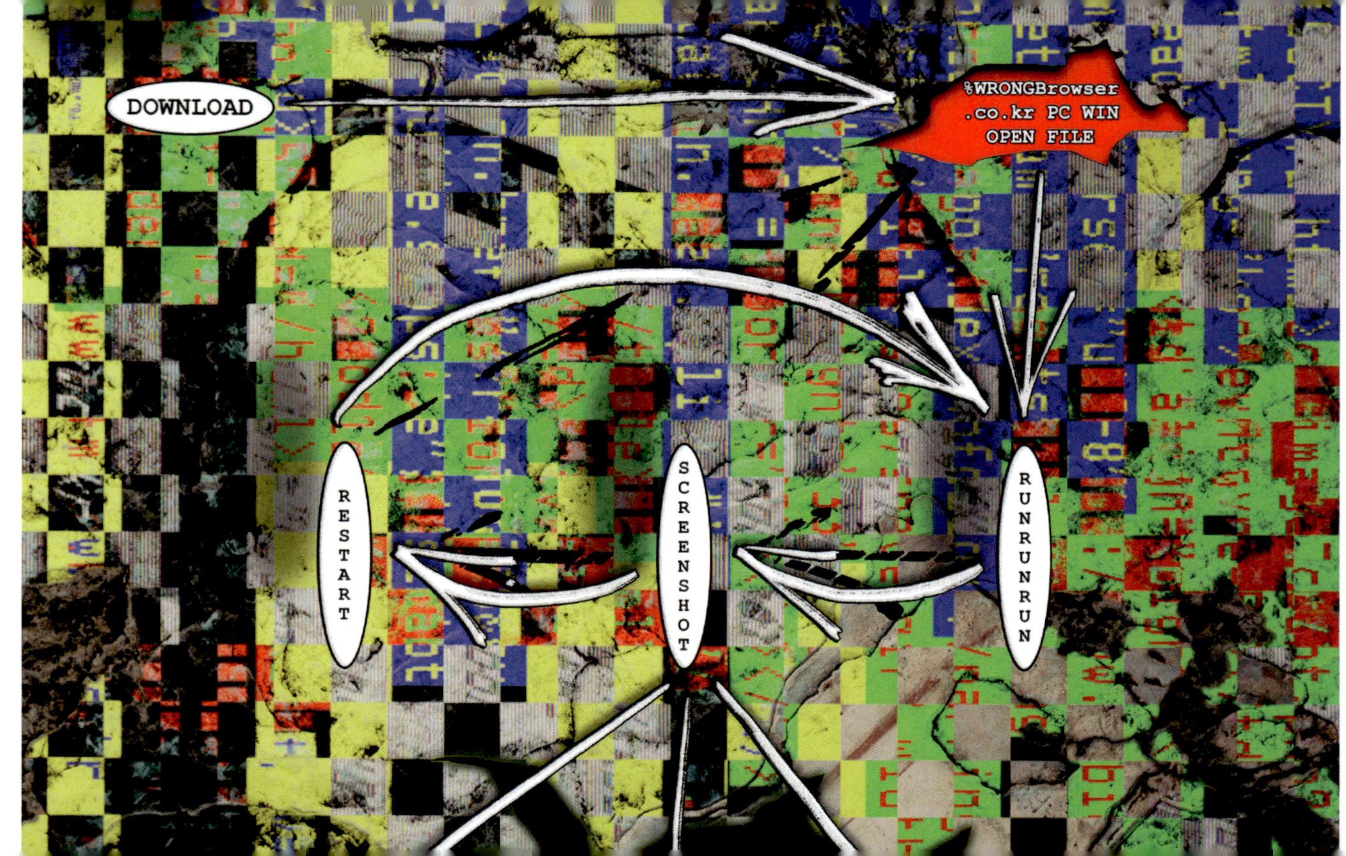
DOWNLOAD
%WRONGBrowser
.co.kr PC WIN
OPEN FILE
RUNRUNRUN
SCREENSHOT
RESTART

SCREENSHOT PROCE|SING BLACKHOLE
CORRECT SCREENSHOT
PARTIAL SCREENSHOT
CORRUPT SCREENSHOT

TECHNOLOGICAL ADVANCEMENT
PROGRAM MALFUNCTION
FRUSTRATION
MISUNDERSTANDINGS
NEW MEANINGS

escape
ever
is
work
no
no
can
its
work
outsideness
as
finished

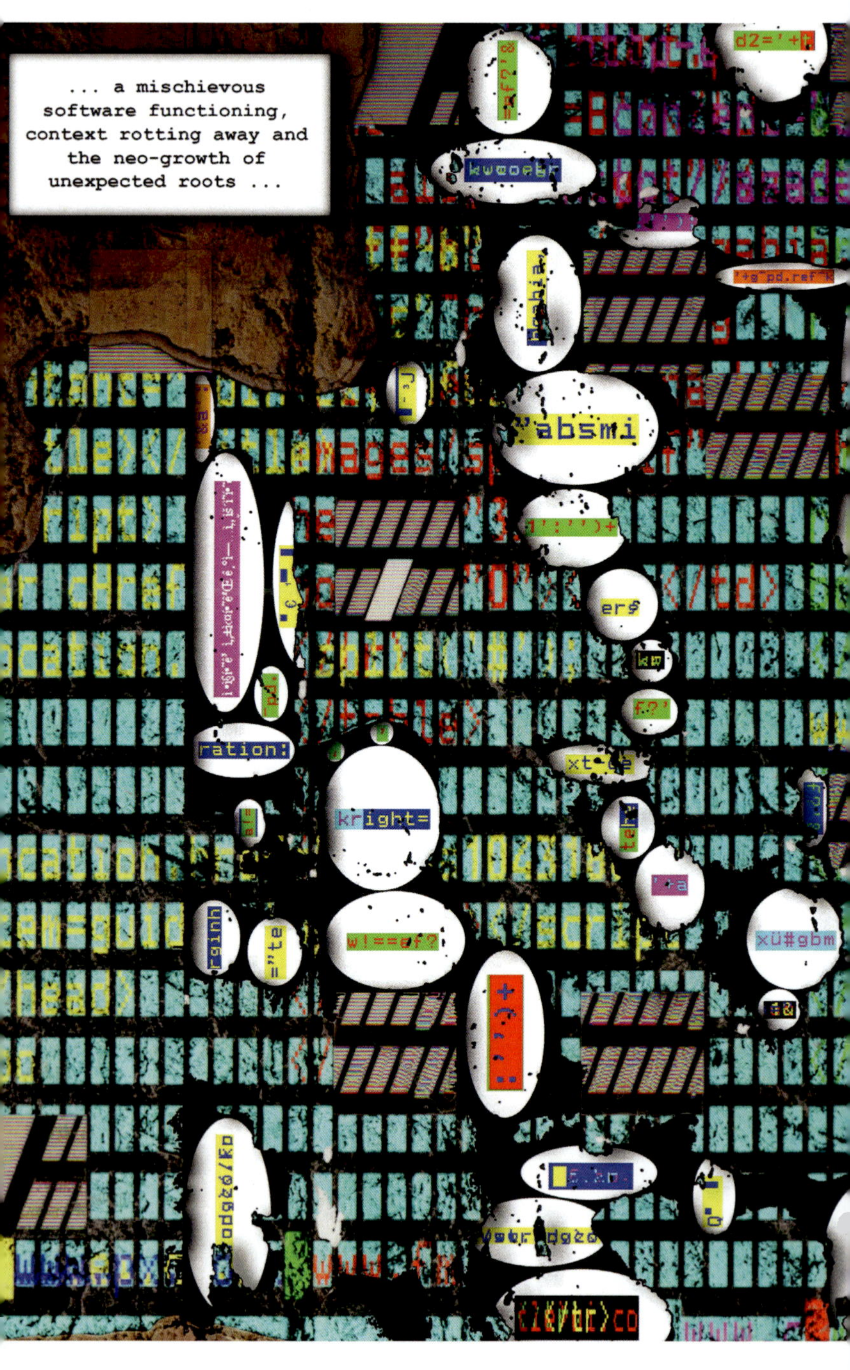
... a mischievous software functioning, context rotting away and the neo-growth of unexpected roots ...

asdasdasdasasasasdasdasdasdasdad
www.kd.co.kr
www.la.co.kr
www.uf.co.kr

Sonia Fizek

Reading Between the Lines. JODI's %WRONG Browser.co.kr

A First-Person Perspective "Meta-Game"

1. I am opening JODI's *%WRONG Browser* website in the current browser of my choice. In 2021, when this experiment is taking place, Safari or Google Chrome are the two largest browsers in popular use.

2. I am downloading the *.co.kr* version of *%WRONG Browser* to my computer's local hard disc. Having installed the software, I struggle to open it. My latest MacOS operating system is no longer compatible with a 32-bit application. I turn to an older machine, which has not seen an update since 2016.[1] This time, I am able to open the application and start the actual "game of browsing".

3. I sit back and watch a neon-like dance of backgrounds and code lines, trying to point and click, write or perform any other actions a user would expect of a standard web browser, such as inputting random text and hitting the return (or enter) button to confirm the command. I use digital, gaming and systemic literacies to interact with the program; all three terms describe an ability to interact with digital systems and their conventions. I am not successful. The browser does not react in a predictable manner to any of my attempts. It does not display or "search" the text input. In most cases, it does not seem to react to clicking either. Its visual interface remains a metaphorical puzzle. JODI's *%WRONG Browser .co.kr* does not "live" a conventional life. I decide to use my imagination instead.

1 The older Macintosh computer ran the following system: OS X Yosemite, Version 10.10.5.

4. To keep the results comparable to one another, I participate in the code spectacle for a few minutes, exit the *%WRONG Browser* and launch it again. And again. I choose to focus on three interaction sessions as method of handling the software in a quasi-laboratory setting. Each time I access the browser, I try to repeat the same actions.

5. I take screenshots to document the digital voyage in the hope of discerning some patterns of code behavior meaningful enough for a later analysis.

6. While watching the *%WRONG Browser* spectacle, I ponder about the meaning of the term "to browse". Etymologically, "to browse" dates back to 15th century Middle English browsen and means "to come into bud" or "to graze". In the late 19th century, the verb started to be used within the context of written media (to browse as in to peruse a book). In the mid-20th century, browsing was extended to electronic digital computers and finally now describes the action of looking for information while going through webpages in the World Wide Web. Browsing has come a long way from literally looking for food to figuratively searching for food for thought, whether in a library, a bound book or online.

The "Game" of Browsing

I am using the term "game" here in a twofold manner; on the one hand, to express my ludic and tinkerer's attitude towards the task of browsing, on the other to describe a methodological approach based on the adaptation of pre-defined rules (e.g. three consecutive browsing sessions; each lasting maximum five minutes and separated by a reset of the program). My interaction with JODI's browser was carried out within the context of a scholarly/art experiment. I was also very conscious of my own role as a researcher/interpreter as well as of JODI art collective. As a result, I was not expecting a predictable standard browsing experience, and in the face of the visual and systemic puzzle of JODI's *%WRONG Browser .co.kr,* I needed a method which would allow me to explore and be creative within a rigid framework. Such an attitude may be interpreted as a ludic one.

Round 1

www.ud.co.kr
The "ud.co.kr" URL is bathing in neon green against a feverishly red background.
www.gi.co.kr
        www.ud.co.kr
Red and black horizontal stripes keep shimmering.
www.gi.co.kr
        www.ud.co.kr
                www.go.co.kr
Black and green horizontal stripes keep shimmering.
www.go.co.kr
        www.ud.co.kr
                www.gi.co.kr
Black and blue horizontal stripes keep shimmering.
www.zu.co.kr
A yellow screen appears with a clock in the right upper corner designating the time "16:57 Uhr".
Black and light blue stripes keep shimmering with the date 2021 displayed in the upper right corner.
www.fi.co.kr
        www.yu.co.kr
Screen turns predominantly black with a few URLS juxtaposed on top of one another.

Round 2 (after reset)

www.py.co.kr

The URL appears in bright green against black background with a red rectangle in the top line of the screen

www.py.co.kr

www.f1.co.kr

Black and red horizontal stripes keep shimmering.

www.f1.co.kr

The URL shines in red against the background composed of black and green horizontal stripes. Two other URL addresses are juxtaposed on top of each other so that their destination is not easily discernible.

www.kd.co.kr

Black and blue horizontal stripes keep shimmering. An incomplete time designation "...4 Uhr" is displayed in the upper right corner.

www.uf.co.kr

www.hz.co.kr

www.nk.co.kr

www.fl.co.kr

The date "10.2021" is displayed in the upper right corner: "hz.co.kr" in purple, "nk.co.kr" in green and "fl.co.kr" in red, all standing out clearly against a dazzling yellow background. Pitch black screen appears and can be covered with white lines of natural language.

My text reads: "asdasdasdasasasasdasdadsda Home Home"

The screen turns into a black and red grid then goes back to dazzling yellow.

The browser freezes in a yellow state of ambience.

A selection of WRONG URLs

www.ij.co.kr
www.hs.co.kr
www.cq.co.kr
www.ez.co.kr
www.kx.co.kr
www.la.co.kr
www.ij.cc
www.jv.co.kr
www.dk.co.kr
www.be.cc.cr
www.vs.co.cr
www.Ij.co.kr
www.mf.co.kr
www.fd.co.kr
www.kn.co.kr
www.ov.kr
www.vb.co.kr

Reflecting Images in Operation

Frieder Nake once wrote in The Algorithmic Art Manifesto: "we cannot see the digital. nor can we hear or smell or taste or touch it. the digital does not exist for human senses. we just cannot perceive it."[2] JODI's *%WRONG Browser* experiment pushes me to go beyond my humanness, as if promising to make me see what usually cannot be seen. Instead of text, images and standard interface elements, I am thrown into a random universe of dazzling code lines. The usual point-and-click visual browsing experience turns into a spectacle of images in operation. In JODI's work, it is the computable or

2 Frieder Nake: Algorithmic Art Manifesto. In: Andrea Sick (ed.): Nevertheless. 17 Manifestos. Hamburg 2018, pp.69-72, here p.69, http://17.manifestos.de/ [accessed 15.6.2022].

the operational that has been moved to the surface for my eyes to see. And although the visual layer has been laid bare, by no means has the digital image become any clearer. The aesthetic of error and operationality turns out to be as muddling as the commercial visual metaphor. In other words, although I laid my eyes on the subface (Ger. Unterfläche) of the twofold image (to lean on Frieder Nake's concept again; Ger. das doppelte Bild), it turned out to be as incomprehensible as scratching its surface (Ger. Oberfläche), if not more so.

The above discovery should not come as surprise. Although the image is digital and discrete, the reception of it must remain analogue and continuous.[3] As a human, I am able to visually judge only the continuous aspect, so the discrete essence of the image needs to be displayed as if it were no different to the traditional analog image. Seeing behind the digital veneer without the ability to read code for its meaning rarely leads to any revelations. To my eye, the operationality of the digital image remains distant and undecipherable.

My short reference to Nake's theory of digital imagery within the context of JODI's *%WRONG Browser* is actually quite natural as the experience of interacting with the browser is a highly visual one. Every line of text and/or code is displayed on the screen and thrown against a brightly pulsating digital canvas. After all, the history of browsing and interacting with electronic computers is a history of human and computer vision. And although other senses have also been engaged in the process (more recently, together with the prevalence of virtual audio assistants such as Apple's Siri, the auditive operationality of media has entered into popular use), vision is usually the starting point for the working with software. In my interpretation, thus, it is impossible not to take the visual aspect into consideration.

3 Frieder Nake: Das doppelte Bild. In: Horst Bredekamp, Matthias Bruhn & Gabriele Werner (eds.): Digitale Form. Bildwelten des Wissens. Kunsthistorisches Jahrbuch für Bildkritik. Berlin 2006.

Fig. 3, Screenshot.

Art tends to make the materiality of the medium particularly striking. It has the capacity to bring its most fundamental aspects to light. And this is the only "stable truth" I am able to hold on to while attending to *%WRONG Browser .co.kr*. Confronted with random visual confusion, I search for understanding and the comfort of usability in the safety of visual theory. I find some consolation in Vilém Flusser's theory of technical image.[4] Flusser rethinks the image vis-à-vis its traditional representational character. Technical images no longer represent or signify any objects found in reality. They construct reality. They do not depict but visualize, model and simulate. For Flusser, although the human observer is not able to see behind the digital veneer, they remain a central figure in the act of "watching" as it is only the human, who has the capacity to turn technical images back into images in

4 Cf. Vilém Flusser: Into the Universe of Technical Images. Minneapolis 2011, p. 33. English translation of: Ins Universum der technischen Bilder (first published in 1985).

the first place. Flusser's interpretation of the human observer has allowed me to shift the understanding of my own role vis-à-vis *%WRONG Browser .co.kr.* I stopped expecting any predictable return messages and did not even attempt to understand the browser's operations. Instead, I turned JODI's browser back into an art performance, which escapes all conventions, even if their existence may have seemed implied by the term "browser". Having initially attempted to understand the undecipherable set of visual operations, I ended up simply appreciating the visual confusion. The truth lies in the beauty of the digital performance.

In Flusser's reflections on the critical reception of the technical image, the question of distance remains central. He sees it as necessary to create new criteria to be used in the analysis of technical images. And these are fundamentally different to the ones familiar from the traditional realm. Since technical images are no longer representations of the outside world but approximations and models of reality, their "critical reception [...] demands a level of consciousness that corresponds to the one in which they are produced".[5]

The meaning of a technical image then is literally encoded. In order to decode a technical image, as Flusser argues, we do not need to read what it shows but rather read how it has been programmed:

We must criticize technical images on the basis of their program. We must start not from the tip of the vector of meaning but from the bow from which the arrow was shot. Criticism of technical images requires an analysis of their trajectory and an analysis of the intention behind it. And this intention lies in the link, the suture of the apparatus that produced them with the envisioners who produced them.[6]

5 Ibid., p. 22.

And precisely this aspect leaves me empty-handed. My documentation of the *%WRONG Browser* rests on the method of close reading that is well-established in literary theory; one which speaks to my human sense of aesthetic and understanding, but one which is not able to penetrate the logic of encoded screen. To understand JODI's browser for future generations is not to read it closely, but at a distance, following in the footsteps of Flusser and more contemporary critical code studies, reading code for more than what it does and focusing instead on its meaning.[7] The unreadability of the browser is not due to its missing code, but to its subversive "nature" as a work of art. Its lack of predictability and conventionality makes it virtually impossible (if not futile) to interpret in accordance with digital industry standards. JODI's browser is an artistic experiment playing with the well-established and popular practice of Internet browsing. We can, or should, thus, question the purpose documenting and archiving this "browser" on the same premises as usability software.

Having reflected on my own act of interpretation, I come back to "browsing". Round three. Attempt three. Reset complete.

Round 3 (after reset)

<*HTML* element> (Code reading)

</strong> *(An html tag defining an important piece of text in the document. In our case the opening tag <strong> is missing, so the tag has no operational meaning)*

 (An HTML element responsible for displaying a line break in text. In our case, there is no text to break. The line is empty. The meaning cannot be broken.)

6 Ibid., p. 48.
7 Cf. Mark C. Marino: Critical Code Studies. Cambridge/MA 2020.

</div> *(In HTML a generic container for flow content. There is no content preceding the tag. It cannot contain.)*
</td> *(An HTML element defining a cell in a table. Where is the table?)*
</tr> *(An HTML element defining a row in the table. It seems there is a table with a cell containing an image; most probably depicting either an autumn landscape, or something else I cannot see.)*
<td><img src="static/images/1/fall04.jpg"
alt="hosting.kr"> </t
</tr> *(An HTML element defining a row in the table)*
</table> *(An HTML tag defining a table)*
</body> *(An HTML tag defining the document's body. This tag is closing a body, there is no opening tag to be found. A full stop, which does not close any sentence.)*
</html>
Empty tags.
Empty containers.
A surface of the subface.
Representation over computation.
Meaningless HTML tags.

My attempt to read the code for what it does reveals that is has no function whatsoever. The HTML tags are used randomly, displayed as images. The "real" code of JODI's *%WRONG Browser* must be buried beneath the neon code veneer. *.co.kr* is a simulation, but one evoking its pre-modern meaning. It remains an encoded optical illusion.

I remain confused.
The subface turns out to be the surface simulating the subface.
I exit the program.

DOI: 10.5282/ubm/epub.93529

Fig. 4, Screenshot.

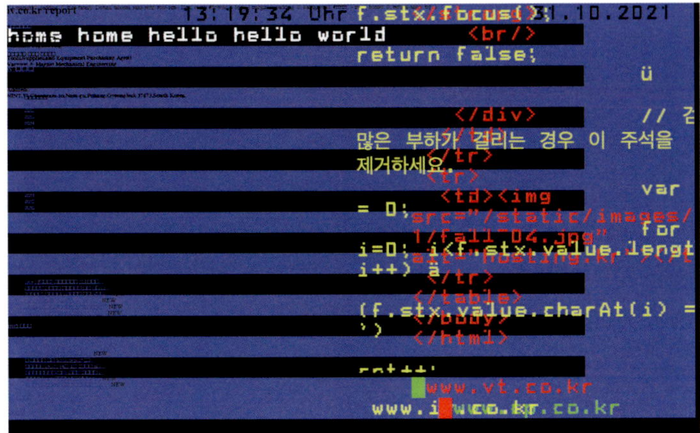

Fig. 1, Handwritten Sketches by the author.

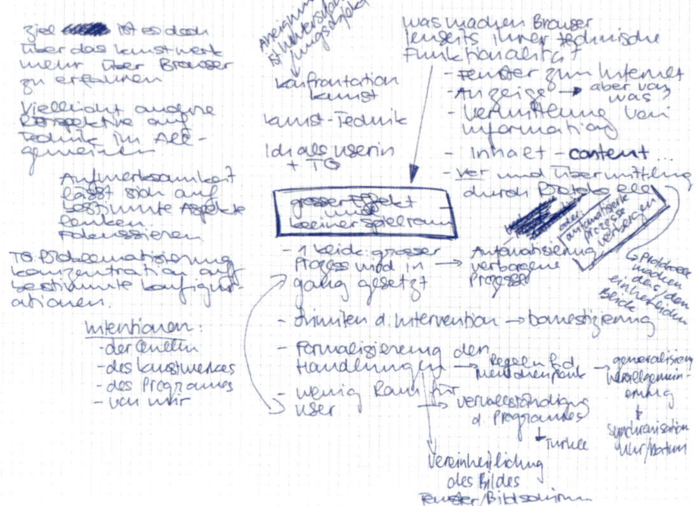

Mirjam Mayer

Process on Display. Navigating through Flashing Light

As a historian, one is used to obscurity. Every investigation begins with a mountain of disorganized sources and the attempt to find orientation. The obscurity as it presented itself in the *%WRONG Browser* was therefore not particularly worrying. From a disciplinary point of view, one could assume that sooner or later a system would come to light, an order could be created, or at least reasons for the confusing composition could be formulated. More disconcerting was the task itself. As a historian of technology, I saw myself confronted with three challenges. They provide the structure for this text.

The first one was the research question. It required that I document how I appropriated the browser and then reflect on that appropriation – all from my standpoint as a historian of technology. The assignment thus oscillated between editing the program as a source through source criticism and writing a source along the lines of a working report of the kind that historians of technology so often find in their source collections. I edited one source to create another. It is likely that this circumstance arises more often than one would like to believe (1). A second difficulty is directly related to the first. It involves an unavoidable personal union. Software programs, be they works of art or not, function as a composition of different components. The user is always part of this composition.[1] In addition to the task of interpreting a source and creating one, there is the unavoidable circumstance of being a user and

1 Cf. Friedrich Kittler: Grammophon - Film - Typewriter. Berlin 1986.

a historian at the same time. That is, I am part of the configuration I am investigating. This might also happen more often that one would like (2). These doublings continue in the third aspect, which revolves around the central object of the task, the browser. This is, on the one hand, a computer program subject to a certain functionality that needs to be seen through, and, on the other hand, an art object that in turn has its own system of reference. The three challenges are obviously circular. It will be the browser itself that subverts these attempts for differentiation (3).

(1) There are no specific guidelines for recording systems in historical scholarship. One excerpts, makes notes and sketches, and perhaps occasionally writes a coherent, structured section of text. Apart from source criticism, there is a relatively wide methodological freedom. The type of research documentation varies and may or may not depend on the object of study. It is often subject to personal preference and habit. In my case, circumstances coincided with customs. The *%WRONG Browser .co.kr* made a totalitarian claim. The program filled the entire screen and allowed no other activity on the device it was running on. The user's view was reduced to this one program.[2] I had to resort to another medium for contemporaneous documentation.

My documentation consists of several handwritten notes and sketches on loose sheets of paper (Fig. 1). At first, I took notes during each short session on the browser. Later I would draw sketches. In these sketches, it is no longer possible to reconstruct a chronology, because they are successively condensed. Simultaneous observation, early associations and researched information spatially entered into direct proximity. I reworked old sketches and broke off current records after only a short time. Some sketches are overviews, others focus on a

2 To see how unconventional this is: Sherry Turkle: Life on the Screen. Identity in the Age of the Internet. New York 1995, p. 14.

specific aspect. Again and again, I started anew, transferring keywords from older sheets and trying to make connections with new observations and thoughts. Thus, my approach was one of constantly writing down, attempting to sort different aspects and relate them to each other. The point was to create orientation through arrangement. The distinction between observation, analysis and association is not marked in this kind of documentation. In a later step, in which I produced a narrative recording of my approach, these different qualities had to be segmented again. Unquestionably, this resulted in further sketches. Basically, the recording system consisted of creating order and destroying it, in order to then begin the sorting work again under new auspices and with new input.

(2) These records provide a basis for distinguishing the four work steps with which I acquired the program. They took place in parallel at almost all times. As a user of the 21st century, it was obvious for me to look for intervention possibilities. Unconcernedly I clicked, deleted and searched for input fields. In keeping with the task at hand, however, I also took stock and tried to differentiate components. Out of personal and professional interest, I read into the brief history of the browser and tried to understand how conventional browsers work.[3] I kept recombining this disparate data to try to form a coherent picture of the browser.

When I first opened it, I was just an observer. I let it run and observed what happened. I documented the aspects that caught my attention. It was overwhelming. I copied down words I saw on the screen and described the components and what they were doing.

Without any intervention, it flashed and sounded. Sounds resembling data processing rang out. Code-like blocks of text ran in different colors and overlapped. The speed of the running

3 Cf. Janet Abbate: Inventing the Internet. Cambridge 2000; David Gugerli. Wie die Welt in den Computer kam. Zur Entstehung digitaler Wirklichkeit. Frankfurt am Main 2018, p. 185; as well as in blogs like the one from Pavel Panchekha & Chris Harrelson: Browsers and the Web. https://browser.engineering/intro.html [accessed 15.6.2022].

blocks varied. Web addresses in different colors appeared at the bottom of the screen. Sometimes they disappeared. Sometimes new ones laid themselves directly over existing addresses. From time to time, a black grid stretched across a good two-thirds of the screen, and illegibly formatted text appeared in the background. At the top of the screen, the current date and the exact time were indicated in black letters. Individual components lit up from time to time. The background constantly changed color. No component could claim its own place on the screen. There were overlaps everywhere. Sometimes characters disappeared in the background of the same color.

After some time the observer became a user. To study the browser, it was not possible to work at a distance from my source. Technologies are almost never closed compositions. Rather, they are specific configurations that produce effects that transcend their representational nature. This task did not allow me to be just a historian of technology. I have been a user of browser software all my life. Experience accompanied custom. As a user, I began to tinker and thus explore my own possibilities for intervention. This quest was exploratory and unstructured. I clicked and double-clicked, moved the mouse and pressed buttons. The user interface changed as I clicked on addresses at the bottom of the screen. It seemed as if this kicked the browser into gear. The blinking increased, the noise became more pervasive, and the colored blocks of code in the foreground ran faster. Dragging and dropping also made it possible to move the addresses around. As the web addresses moved, so did the code blocks. Moving the addresses revealed their connection to the code. They belonged to the same page. Such a code could now be viewed individually by removing the overlap of the blocks. Using the arrow keys of the keyboard, the running of the codes could be slowed down and almost stopped. Furthermore, it was possible to write into the colored codes, to change or delete lines. Outside the code blocks, one could write across the entire screen, starting from the top left. The text then appeared in black letters between the code blocks and the black grid. The codes obscured the text input thus generated, and the grid provided a poor background for good readability of the black text.

While searching for input locations, different levels of the browser became visible. The top level was the web addresses at the bottom and the associated code blocks. Behind it was a writable area that became visible only through my input, which in turn had no effect on program activity. Behind it stretched the black grid. Although it disappeared briefly in the blinking of the program, it seemed to mark a boundary beyond which there were no more input possibilities. On this rearmost level was simply formatted text. It was barely legible, changed by itself and was replaced from time to time. The way the text was extended or replaced by a new one seemed like the result of a loading process – always accompanied by the sound of data processing.

(3) The indication of the current time and date at the top of the screen caught my attention early on. It looked like the title of the work. The browser was obviously synchronized and not a relic of history. It was always committed to the present and constantly up to date. The browser set the pace. The timing seemed to convey that the processes were always running. They could no more be stopped than the passage of time. By taking up the whole screen, the program window imposed its specific interface on the user without giving her any free space. This is probably as true for the *%WRONG Browser* as for a conventional one. The display of the web page is relative to its code. But browsers determine the possibility of representability and visibility.

One of the first impulses was to enter the web addresses in a conventional browser and look up the pages they led to. It was a South Korean domain. The footer of the *.co.kr* addresses identified the location of the data and indicated commercial use. Many of the websites were no longer in operation, some led to the same websites, and most of the websites that were still active were themselves selling commercially usable web addresses from a South Korean domain. The web pages corresponded with the texts displayed at the backmost level of the *%WRONG Browser*. Underlining, words, numbers and mail addresses indicated similarities between the content of the web pages and the text in the background of the program. Here, the content had almost nothing to do with the shape of the web pages as they presented themselves in a conventional browser. The content was barely structured and eluded the usefulness of conveying information. In essence, the program reversed conventional browser activity. Browsers are commonly used to display web pages from a network. In the case of the *%WRONG Browser*, it is the HTML versions of the web pages that are foregrounded in the form of colorful and glancing blocks of code. Clicking on a web address loads the page to the backmost level of the browser. The sound reminiscent of processing marks this data transfer.

Through tinkering and a little enquiry, the space that the program had opened structured itself. The browser was set up. Interventions were possible. Things could be written, deleted and moved. However, not all of my interventions seemed to have a comprehensible effect. Calling up web pages by clicking on the addresses was the only thing that led to a noticeable effect. In most cases, there was no comprehensible coherence between input and output.[4]

4 See here that this is rather common for digital media from the perspective of the user: Cornelia Vismann: Akten. Medientechnik und Recht. Frankfurt am Main 2000, p. 300.

Fig. 2, Synchronizing with the %WRONG Browser at the kitchen table.

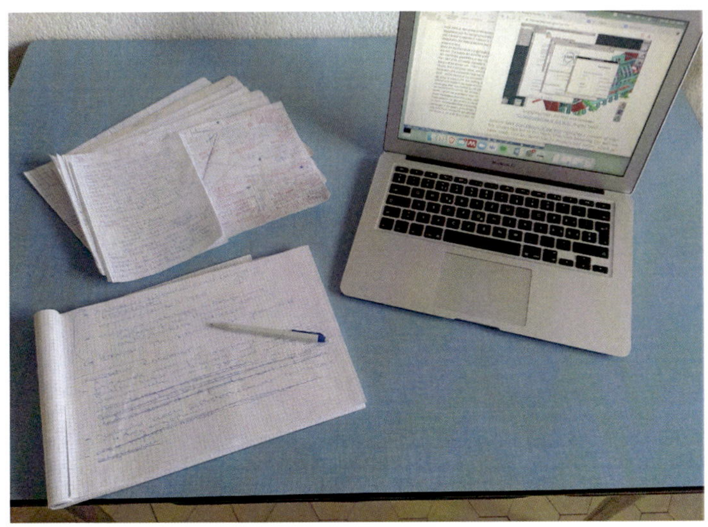

By bringing processes to the foreground that otherwise remained invisible, the browser produced obscurity. However, this activated my willingness as a user to act to find orientation. It may seem that usability is not the focus of this browser, because one's own position and ability to act are not immediately apparent. The view is reversed and the possibilities for intervention are small. The mechanisms of user guidance, however, are not very different from those of conventional browsers. Users sound out their options, follow the cues of a particular composition, and let the program direct their attention based on their experience with other software programs. The autonomous user constantly falls back on proven patterns.

Fig. 1, Illustration of the author's meandering research process. The darker yellow areas show roughly the sequence of actions, starting at the top left. While not every micro step is entered here, the illustration should provide information about which questions and observations were made on the grounds of which empirical data.

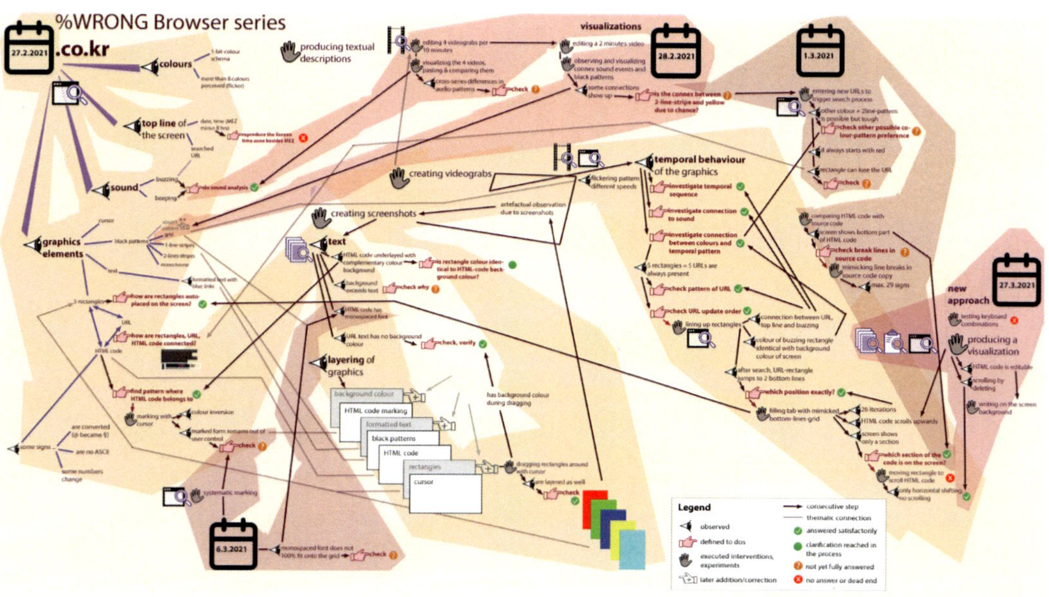

Inge Hinterwaldner

Meta-forensics: Is it possible to get %WRONG Browser right?

My task was to get to know the browser as well as possible, to document it in a way that would enable someone who did not have the chance to interact with the application to get a feel for it. For me, that involves pictorial densification and narration, taking the reader of the documentation – that tightly interlaces images and text – by the hand and leading them through the jungle of impressions and opportunities for interaction.

Biases

First, I must address some biases, which somewhat compromised my contribution with respect to a "clean" set of experiments as envisioned in this issue.

Pre-knowledge due to interviews with the artists.
The documentation of *.co.kr* was the fourth documentation I have made of JODI's *%WRONG Browser* series. In total, I dealt with: .com.mx, .nl, .cn, [interviews on 1/26/2021 and 2/12/2021], *.co.kr, .com,* and *.br,* in this order. The last three of these were informed in several ways by conversations with the artist duo. I took the nomenclature and responded to clues either by dropping the follow-up of a (clarified) detail or by deepening the investigation (if discrepancies are suspected).

Pre-knowledge due to analysing a series.
The browsers in the series have some design elements in common. Therefore, the aspects that had been explored in detail in another browser were only briefly verified in the next, placed well down on the list of priorities, or used en passant as a given to target something else. The epistemic significance had thus changed.

Main questions

My central questions are: a) How are the elements or phenomenological aspects related to each other? b) What patterns can be found (to ask later: how can they be interpreted?)? This inquiry model allows me to adopt a low-level entry point in the sense that I can begin basically anywhere, my attention can refer to tiny connections which can then accumulate, cluster and thus enable me to recognize larger complexes. These build on former observations and thus, as the analysis advances, my analysis becomes ever more entangled with the specific artwork in question.

Hardware and software

I mostly worked with two monitors (laptop and a larger external monitor) simultaneously, which allowed me to have the browser running, filling the whole screen of monitor 1, and have a window open next to it for the several other programs I use. When working with only one monitor, I switched between the programs with alt+tab. Generally – for better screenshots – I try to run the browsers on a larger monitor (which did not work in this case). This was the only hardware-related consideration I brought to the documentation, otherwise my tools remained limited to software. I used the following programs:

- Mozilla Firefox 78.2.0esr (64-Bit) for comparing HTML- and source code
- Greenshot for full screen screenshots
- IrfanView 32 to view screenshots
- Bandicam 4.5.6.1647 for screen recording
- MiniTool MovieMaker 2.0 for editing videos
- VLC Media Player for watching videos
- Sonic Visualizer 4.2 for visualizing sound in video
- Adobe Photoshop 2020 for creating visualizations (besides pen and paper)
- Word in Microsoft Office Professional Plus 2019 for textual documentation

From a nonlinear process towards a linear documentation

In the documentation I set three priorities: a) to map my explorative procedure, b) record my days of analysis, c) ensure consistency in the reading flow of the illustrated Word document along the aspects I studied. These three dimensions could only be combined with compromises (Fig. 1).

I start the process of familiarizing myself with an 'autopilot'-program like *.co.kr* by first simply observing it before moving into an interactive engagement. In the first phase, I mostly use screen recording (screenshots to a lesser extent). Here, I make a broad variety of observations and register these mentally. After about ten minutes, I start to write down what I have found. I describe the points and initial patterns I observe and put these into a (text-induced) linear order. In this initial stage of collecting impressions, the order is not yet a major concern. It is more important that nothing is forgotten, and everything is filed as 'seeds' that can be developed as individual nuclei at a later stage.

Exploration.
Initially, the screenshots serve as evidence for referencing the many details that remain constant. The description of this inventory is created anew with each application and is not oriented according to a preconceived list. Even entities of the next higher level of complexity, that is performative patterns, are the results of my conceptualizations, and thus usually cannot be revealed in the same way via screenshots. Sometimes, it turns out that an observation is declared as a pattern too early, that a tentative explanation seems to be implausible after all, or that an aspect has been looked at only imprecisely or partially. This is often the case while the events are too confusing. Only gradually does it become possible to isolate the simultaneous events and to observe them individually. At this point, the phase of conceptual clustering for the observation and documentation begins. The individual events and patterns are then labelled with descriptive names of my own invention (here for example the 'black pattern'). This process of isolation is necessary for the analysis, in order to understand the interaction of the elements and to grasp this as a synthesis. Once this is understood, test series are set up. One strategy for mining information in works with parallel and autonomous processes is by going to extremes, provoking singularities, that is producing a stress test of the application. I find this particularly appealing because the range of the program's processes would appear to be a meaningful metric. Exploring the limits and conditions of the possibilities for expression paves the way for an exploratory, criminalistic or forensic procedure. A second strategy is to create 'clean' situations to get an unobstructed

'view'. Depending on the application at hand, this can either take the form of a restart, of 'emptying' the screen or of inducing an easily recognizable pattern, from which the subsequent deviation is suspected to be informative.

Consolidation.

Initially, I gather impressions from every direction before going on to expand them, consolidate them, determine their scope, and possibly explain them. At this point, at the latest (here from day 2), the linearity of the textual documentation necessarily begins to diverge from the procedure. I start by noting down my observations and trying to clarify the open questions in the examination of the application selectively (this is where the reddish arms point to in Fig. 1).

Structuring the documentation.

The key task now is to structure the documentation text. For better orientation, the paragraphs are retrospectively provided with bold headings or text passages that indicate their own conceptual clusters. This allows me to insert subsequent additional information more quickly and in the correct place. Cross-references of a different kind run down the text via asterisks (* that indicate answers to previously posed questions) and via the numbered trials. Things that are still unclear are marked in red as questions, because even knowing what you do not know is helpful. Sometimes I deliberately and openly admit that I am in conversation with my earlier observations, the assessment of which may have changed several times, because the information that there was confusion here can also be significant.

Trials – or test series – are deliberately created and executed experimental arrangements with the browser. Not all confrontations with the browser are declared as experiments. Which of them are listed as such is relatively contingent upon whether an explanation is required of how a result was reached or the complexity of the step. Pure exact observation does not qualify as an 'experiment', excursions with external analysis tools do. The experimental setups are intuitively designed to address the general guiding questions above. My experimental set-up design is not always right, sometimes the test series needs to be longer or have a different resolution. Fig. 2, for instance, is successful as micro patterns become evident. However, long-term patterns do not yet come into view as the sample is too short.

In the experiments, I more often take screenshots than use screen recording. Here, I am consciously not yet very specific, the screenshots aim at a phenomenological range, at difference in color, form and composition, or try to capture (supposed) peculiarities. The screenshots are also discussed ever more specifically later in the documentation text. This is in keeping with the spirit of the procedure as a whole. In this post-initial phase, where I 'look' a bit more thoroughly, I still make a lot of casual observations, but this decreases successively as I gradually clarify the various aspects. The investigative gaze becomes both sharper and narrower. In cases where the perception of a particularity (such as a suspected bug or Easter egg) becomes more pronounced, I direct the reader's attention with the help of detail screenshots, which are practically always incorporated into the Word document and annotated. Otherwise only a small selection of screenshots of the whole monitor find their way into the text document and the remainder are simply filed in a folder.

Fig. 2, Attempt to clarify the temporal correlation between the buzzing and beeping sound (waveform diagram, 2 minutes) and the black patterns in the color-coded stripe on top.

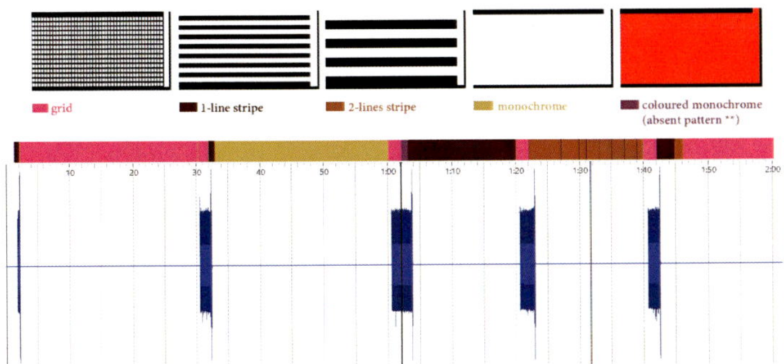

Visualizations.
Being aware of recognizing and remembering visual elements better than time-based features, I put a special focus on the latter a) by repeating a situation in a targeted manner so that a specific dynamic is staged for the video grab and b) by producing visualizations. The visualizations are intended to be condensed clarifications of connections and can compile cumulative events in a proto-statistical manner (lots of counting!) or combine different features of an individual (typical) runtime section (Fig. 3).

This connects to Franco Moretti's "artificial constructs" that present information in an abstract model to create a sharper sense of how elements are connected.[1] In addition, visualizations are useful for explaining relationships that are recognized during the inquiry but cannot be captured with screenshots alone. The collage (Fig. 4) is intended to make clear that the screen view shows only a section of the bigger picture. To

1 Franco Moretti: Graphs, Maps, Trees. Abstract Models for a Literary History. London 2005, p. 1.

Fig. 3, Comparative line-up of waveform diagrams (10 minutes) from four different works of JODI's %WRONG Browser series in order to determine whether the sound (search) events exhibit different patterns.

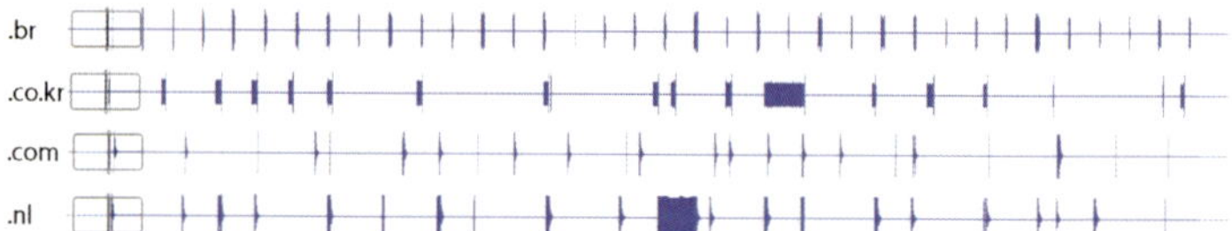

depict the off-screen elements, I do not shy away from inventing fictitious HTML code sections that are visually plausible or copied from other screenshots. Since JODI's font is custom made, and consequently cannot be found in font libraries, I approximated the font with one that comes close to the original impression (I took *Source Code Variable* (designed by Paul D. Hunt, 2017), bold, 27pt), but leaves the reconstruction recognizable as in a *tratteggio* retouching.

Fig. 1 reveals that the most time-consuming steps – such as these ad hoc visualizations – end up being labelled as having only partial results. This may have something to do with the slight dissatisfaction I feel here, as I can think of many more ways to optimize these visualizations for producing evidence. Here, the orange signs are shorthand for 'it could be improved'.

General features

Varying degrees of depth in analysis.
Evaluating my results critically and in retrospect, it is noticeable that the degree of analysis and time invested in this evaluation work differs according to my biases and the presumed significance of the targeted detail. In some cases, I was even prepared to accept a process as a performative 'pattern' if I was able to

Fig. 4, Speculative completion of the graphical elements that have left the viewport of the screen, respecting the layering order and the formatting of the HTML-codes (left-aligned: red, green, blue; centered: light blue; right-aligned: yellow). The version 'monochrome' was chosen as 'black pattern'.

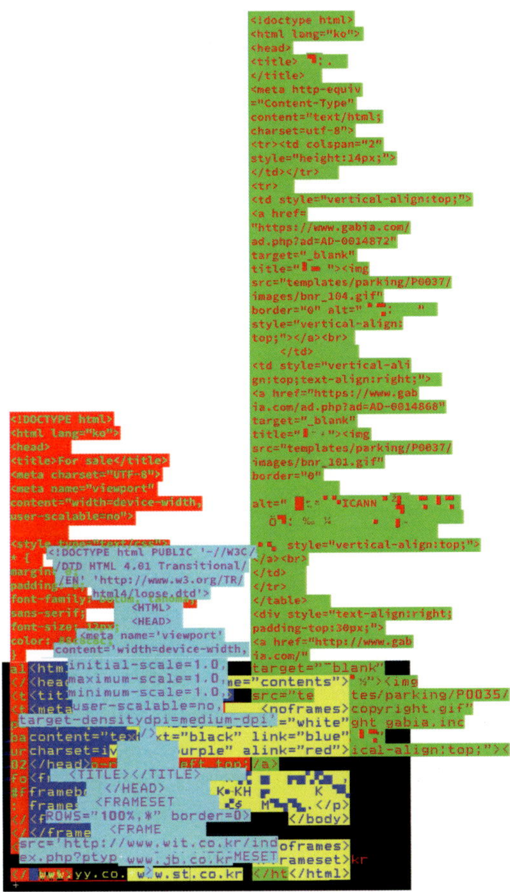

replicate it once (!) or twice, or if it repeated itself. Sometimes, I consider aspects that were only analyzed once but could be 'consolidated' at a second instance as being transferable to other elements. This procedure presupposes that the work is subject to a constant set of rules and that coherence and correlation are predominant. This was unquestioningly assumed in the context of these programmed works. Some aspects

a) were observed, tested, or tracked down until no more questions were open.

b) could be clarified briefly without problems but did not arouse any special curiosity due to the biases mentioned. This was seen as a compulsory exercise and initially pushed into the list "(confident to know how it works but) not yet tried".

c) were taken as given only on the basis of intuitive judgements without being objectified further. For example, I thought the term 'color inversion' was adequate for the marking, even though I did not measure the individual color values.

d) were analytically only teased (such as the long-term pattern in Fig. 2, also indicated as 'semi-clarified' by orange marking in Fig. 1), e.g., if the analysis is very labour-intensive with the present means.

e) were considered a desideratum but not pursued due to a lack of adequate tools, otherwise the process would be too exhausting, fragmentary, or error-prone.

More curiosity-driven than systematic.

The various distinguishable iconographic steps were not systematically separated: oscillating between interaction and analysis, the text documentation mixes simple descriptions, externally researched results and first interpretative approaches. Viewed retrospectively, my style of documentation feels like the beginning of a research project that has stopped midway as it falls short of argumentation, theorization and contextualization. The interpretative bits and pieces are brief and serve to note down the ideas that arose during the investigation, so that they could be used later for academic elaboration. Thus, I would see my outcome as a hybrid. The short inquests 'outside' the *%wrong Browser* – in a 'competitor' browser – were quite relaxing and enabled me to create small packages of information that may well be useful when sorting through the many aspects that are still not understood. It did not occur to me that I could seek out this additional information within *.co.kr,* i.e. to take this browser seriously in its browsing capacity. For this experimental endeavour, however, quite different test arrangements would be needed... which leads me to my final point.

Open-ended.
I interacted with the application until I ran out of ideas of what to do next. Distributing the analysis over several days proved useful as it gave fresh ideas time to emerge. Reading the documentation after an interval of a few days was a valuable exercise as forgetfulness allowed me to detect gaps and insecurities in the own documentation as well as aspects I had only half understood. The production of visualizations is also a valuable testbed for proving a full understanding. Completeness is an aim. This exploratory approach faces a latent 'halting problem' and thus probably a pragmatic ending. Here, the "epistemic thing"[2] feels like a fractal or even rhizome where one can always refine an inquiry even regarding the most unsuspecting occasions and can find another seed or pocket to explore in greater detail. My hope is, however, that the loose ends will grow together, that details will meet in instances of mutual confirmation and become "robust".[3]

DOI: 10.5282/ubm/epub.93573

2 Cf. Hans-Jörg Rheinberger: Experimentalsysteme und epistemische Dinge. Eine Geschichte der Proteinsynthese im Reagenzglas. Göttingen 2001.

3 Cf. William Wimsatt: The ontology of complex systems. Levels of organization, perspectives, and causal thickets. In: Canadian Journal of Philosophy. Biology & Society. Reflections on Methodology, no. 20, 1994, pp. 207-274, here pp. 214-215.

Table 1. Morphological box of JODI's %WRONG Browser .co.kr.

	Dimension	Characteristics							
	Content type	Code	Rendered	Navigation (Link)	Date	Time			
	Interaction possibility	Text Input	Highlight via double click on text	Navigate via double click on button	Escape to end program				
	Trigger	User (external)	Program (internal)						
	Page layout	Navigation area (bottom across)	Date area (top across)	Text input (left side)	Content area (left, center, right)				
	Flicker effect	Highlight	Background	None					
	Sound effect	Click sound (double toot sound)	Loading sound (rattling sound)	Ready sound (simple, longer toot sound)					
	Mouse cursor	Arrow	Cross						
	Graphical object	Black grid	Rectangular buttons						
	Background color	Red	Green	Blue	Yellow	Cyan	Magenta	Black	
Text	Color	Red	Green	Blue	Yellow	Cyan	Magenta	Black	White
Text	Highlight color	Red	Green	Blue	Yellow	Cyan	Magenta	Black	White
Text	Alignment	Left	Center	Right	Justified				
Text	Size	Small	Large						
Text	Motion	Scrolling	None						

Hendrik Wache, Sarah Hönigsberg, Barbara Dinter

How to Capture an ARTifact from the Information Systems Perspective

Problem definition

Digitization is transforming not only traditional businesses and everyday life but also other facets of our society, such as the arts. In business, the issue of legacy systems based on obsolete digital technologies has long been a problem. In art, too, this phenomenon becomes significant when artworks are based on digital technologies that are no longer supported. There is a threat that digital artifacts representing instrumental, aesthetic, and symbolic values in various contexts may be lost, so ways must be found to document and archive them for posterity. The field of Information Systems (IS) has a history not only of developing digital artifacts and analyzing their use, but also of documenting these artifacts and archiving design knowledge. Therefore, the question arises: How can an artistic digital artifact be documented and archived for posterity from an IS perspective? For this purpose, a method, described in terms of a set of steps necessary to perform a task[1], was developed using approaches from the area of design archaeology.[2] The result is demonstrated on JODI's *%WRONG Browser .co.kr.*

1 Salvatore T. March & Gerald F. Smith: Design and Natural Science Research on Information Technology. In: Decision Support Systems, vol. 15, no. 4, 1995: pp. 251–266.

2 Leona Chandra Kruse, Stefan Seidel & Jan vom Brocke: Design Archaeology. Generating Design Knowledge from Real-World Artifact Design. In: Bengisu Tulu, Soussan Djamasbi & Gondy Leroy (eds.): Extending the Boundaries of Design Science Theory and Practice. Cham 2019, pp. 32–45.

Reflection on our approach and description as a method

Our approach to documenting the digital art artifact can be divided into three steps: 1) Contextualizing, 2) Engaging and Describing, and 3) Reflecting and Documenting (Fig. 1). In Step 1, the documenter attempts to understand the artwork in its context. This involves two sub-steps: the initial exploration which examines the type of art artifact present and how to interact with it, and the historical analysis which determines what information is available about the artifact, e.g. through internet research. In addition to gaining an understanding of the context, the documenter also creates an initial fact sheet containing the key information about the digital artifacts. In Step 2, the documenter seeks to build up knowledge about

Fig. 1, Documentation method for an artistic digital artifact.

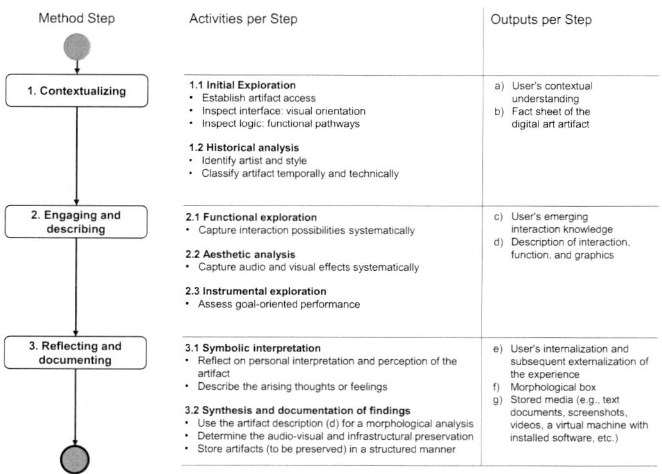

the possibilites for interacting with the artifact through real interaction with the artifact itself and, in parallel, creates an unstructured transcript of the engagement.

This takes place in three sub-steps: an examination of the artifact's functions, a study of its aesthetic elements and, finally, a consideration of its fitness for purpose. Thus, the output of this step is two-fold; on the one hand, the documenter accumulates knowledge and skills for interacting with the artifact, and on the other hand, they create initial unstructured documentation. For example, in the *%WRONG Browser .co.kr* study, documentation includes "clicking colorful buttons in front of web page names → double-clicking to navigate." This step of engaging and describing should be conducted by two people, if possible. That way, one person interacts with the artifact while "thinking out loud", i.e. verbalizing any thoughts in an unfiltered way, so the two people can reflect on the interaction together. This provides the basis for the documentation.

In Step 3 (Reflecting and Documenting), the documenter now also adopts an interpretive approach. First, the functional descriptions of Step 2 are supplemented by the description of the artifact's effect on the viewer. Next, the documenter finally archives the artifact in the optimum format.

An example of the symbolic interpretation notes from the first of these sub-steps was that *%WRONG Browser* triggers "a sense of insecurity or fear of malware" and an "urge to recognize patterns that do not appear to be there." In the second sub-step, the documenter performed a synthesis of all the collected findings. A morphological analysis of the *%WRONG Browser* user interface was conducted for this purpose. The consolidated representation of the artifact in a morphological box (Table 1) enables the reader to think through the possible configurations of the artifact relatively easily, even without having access to the digital artifact. The archiving was done with screenshots (Fig. 2).

During the Reflection process in Step 3, we were able to identify three principles that strongly characterize the design: 1) constant flow, 2) limited agency, and 3) deconstruction of browsing. Constant flow describes how the digital artifact in its various states continuously changes the configuration of the characteristics described in the morphological box, e.g. a change of the background color from green to red. Limited agency highlights the fact that these configuration changes can only be controlled by the user to a limited extent, i.e. many characteristics described in the morphological box cannot be selected by users themselves. Deconstruction of browsing describes how the browsing experience is taken apart so that only text segments, colors, shapes, and sounds remain, which are difficult for the user to navigate and interpret.

Discussion of results

In this paper, a method was developed that allows a documenter to examine and experience a digital artifact of the present while recording it for posterity. In doing so, it was shown that instruments familiar from the IS domain are also transferable to other disciplines that deal with the archiving of knowledge about digital artifacts. Approaches adopted from the area of design archaeology[3] helped us to analyze an existing artifact and capture knowledge about its design. The morphological analysis and presentation of the results in a morphological box[4] assisted us in coping with the complexity of the described artifact.

In our study, we draw on established approaches of the IS discipline by developing a method, using systematization approaches such as morphological boxes, and capturing design

3 Cf. Chandra Kruse, Seidel & vom Brocke.

4 Fritz Zwicky: Discovery, invention, research through the morphological approach, New York 1969.

Fig. 2, Screenshot of JODI's %WRONG Browser .co.kr.

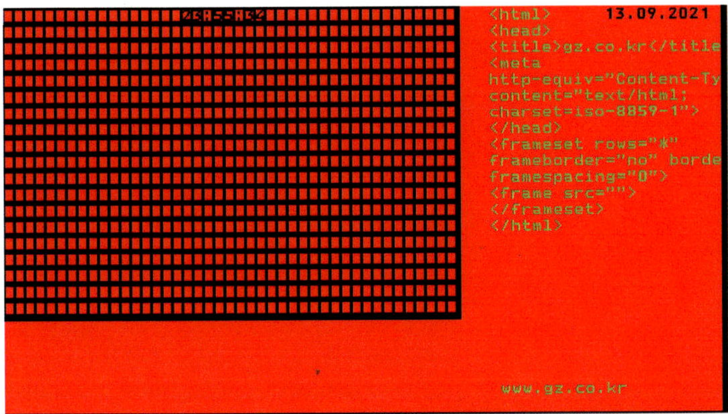

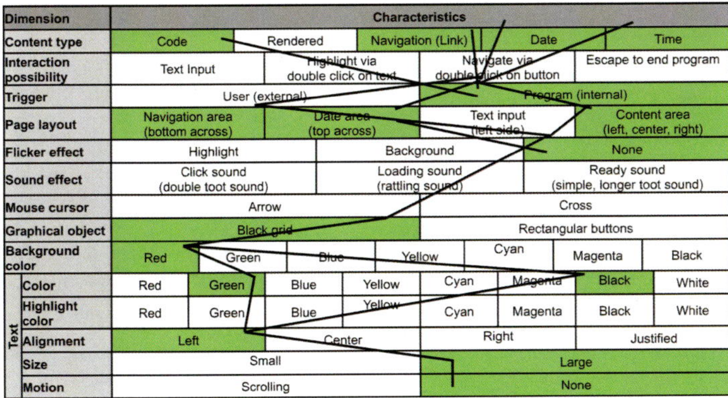

Dimension		Characteristics							
Content type		Code	Rendered	Navigation (Link)	Date	Time			
Interaction possibility		Text Input	Highlight via double click on text	Navigate via double click on button	Escape to end program				
Trigger		User (external)	Program (internal)						
Page layout		Navigation area (bottom across)	Date area (top across)	Text input (left side)	Content area (left, center, right)				
Flicker effect		Highlight	Background	None					
Sound effect		Click sound (double toot sound)	Loading sound (rattling sound)	Ready sound (simple, longer toot sound)					
Mouse cursor		Arrow	Cross						
Graphical object		Black grid	Rectangular buttons						
Background color		Red	Green	Blue	Yellow	Cyan	Magenta	Black	
Text	Color	Red	Green	Blue	Yellow	Cyan	Magenta	Black	White
	Highlight color	Red	Green	Blue	Yellow	Cyan	Magenta	Black	White
	Alignment	Left	Center	Right	Justified				
	Size	Small	Large						
	Motion	Scrolling	None						

Table 2, Example of a configuration in the morphological box to describe a screenshot.

knowledge in design principles. What is new from the IS perspective is that we apply these approaches to digital artifacts already designed and being used. With this, we adopt a new perspective; instead of putting the main focus on actively designing and prescribing, we focus on analyzing and persisting design knowledge.

Capturing digital artifacts through documentation and, where possible, preservation allows subsequent individuals who do not (or no longer) have the opportunity to experience and witness a digital artifact first-hand to learn about it second-hand instead. Second-hand viewing, unfortunately, does not allow later users to experience the social component of a digital artifact or to experience using it individually for themselves. Still, documentation of the technical aspects can allow posterity to engage with the digital artifact, even if it is no longer available. This will enable individuals studying the digital artifact in the future to learn/speculate about its meaning and the experience of using it.

The developed method uses a morphological box to produce the key documentation of the digital artifact. The identified dimensions and characteristics allow the possible states of the artifact to be classified for a better understanding. The combination of the artifact's screenshot (Fig. 2) and morphological box, in which the visible configuration of the artifact is marked off (Table 2), ensures better classification of what can be seen in the image and the possible configurations that have not been captured.

Overall, the developed method helps the documenter to appropriately document and preserve a digital artifact for posterity. Using the research behind this paper, it could be shown that this method was suitable for documenting *%WRONG Browser .co.kr* and that different result types could be generated.

In addition to the morphological box, a further aspect that is of particular importance is ensuring the complete persistence of the digital artifact. This can be achieved using a virtual machine in most cases. However, digital preservation is becoming more difficult with the increasing popularity of distributed digital software (distributed among different computers).

The developed method can be used for the documentation of other digital artifacts beyond *%WRONG Browser .co.kr*. This makes these artifacts comparable, although to a limited extent. Over time, repeated application of the method could be used to collect possible dimensions of different artifacts in a knowledge base, making it increasingly easy to describe new digital artifacts and potentially classify them according to various categories.

As a limitation, it should be noted that the source code of *%WRONG Browser .co.kr* was not available for examination and preservation. Source code is an important aspect of evaluating and interpreting a digital artifact, as analysis of its content allows conclusions to be drawn about decisions made during the design process. Moreover, source code itself is a medium that allows conclusions to be drawn about the programmer's level of knowledge and skill. Even if running an executable file is no longer possible, an analysis of the source code can reconstruct the behavior and presentation of the application to a certain extent.

Furthermore, no evaluation of the method was conducted, and it could not be determined how domain experts, such as art historians, may perceive the added value or usability of the method. As future research, the described method could be compared with approaches from other disciplines and should be evaluated by domain experts.

DOI: 10.5282/ubm/epub.93574

Findings

Users' perspectives (continuation)

Conceptualisation of the assignment and the object of study

As expected, the approaches differed considerably, partly due to the way that each person explicitly or implicitly interpreted the task at hand (document this browser in the best way or develop a framework for documenting all browsers in the best way) and how he or she defined the browser for herself, namely for instance as a digital artefact (Wache et al.), a generic Graphical User Interface (Hönigsberg), a system with meaning and purpose (Hedblom), an epistemic thing and puzzle (Hinterwaldner), an obscurity to be enlightened into a coherent picture (Mayer), a site of multiple diffractions (Mitrokhov), a spectacle and glimpse into the subface (Fizek) or an instance affecting the observer (Dippel).

Methodological adjustments

Most of the contributors reported at least one kind of U-turn in their method, due to a variety of reasons. For Mayer it was the necessity of giving up the distance to the studied source, for Fizek the failing of the hermeneutical approach of close-reading, for Mitrokhov the program running in a buggy way, for Hönigsberg the choice of documentation setup was cumbersome and did not fuse the information as envisioned and the software performance was not compatible with the pre-established structured approach, for Hedblom the own methodology works only with less chaotic systems and for Hinterwalder the choice of documentation led to interpretative mistakes.

While several participants adopted a decidedly analytical approach, some had stronger conceptual filters than others in place: separating syntax from semantics, then breaking down into smaller semantic entities (Hedblom), separating insider and outsider perspectives, then fine-tuning the breaking down and isolating affordances of interaction (Richter); others had a more indeterminate or open way of exploration at first, but then came up with labels for structuring the findings (Wache et al., Hinterwaldner). A third group seemed to go for a more synthesized outcome from the start (Hönigsberg, Dippel). Some chased the ghost of 'completeness' (Hönigsberg, Hinterwaldner, Wache et al.), for others this was not an aim; it might even have been incompatible with the underlying theory (Mitrokhov).

Focus

All contributors had an implicit or explicit focus when conceptualizing the documentation.

For Wache et al. it was guiding design principles and suitability for the purpose of browsing, for Dippel what cultural positions and theories could be linked to the browser's phenomenological dimensions, such as persistence and repetition, for both Dippel and Mitrokhov it was being exposed, for Fizek remaining playful, for Hedblom decomposing the system into an ontological hierarchy in order to end up with small semantic patterns of concepts that could be operationable, for both Hedblome and Richter it was identifying the interconnectivity between components and their purpose or performative patterns for Hinterwaldner, for Hönigsberg showing the application behaviour through targeted user interventions with a GUI (Hönigsberg) and for Mitrokov it was contingency of (dys)functionality.

Many centred a good portion of their attention on the scope of interactivity: some did this in general terms with less preforming guidelines (Mayer), some strived for a more specific stance, for instance opening up ludic or creative kinds of intervention (Fizek), viewing it as a situated and embodied experience (Mitrokhov) or performing paratactically more normalized interventions (Hönigsberg, Richter) suitable for repetition or verifiability respectively.

These differences were the immediate findings that grabbed our attention when we received the contributions. To further discuss what we could learn about this methodological experiment, we held an authors' workshop on March 25, 2022. Our aim was to address questions such as: what did we learn about documentation from considering navigation as a method? What did we learn about the artists' browsers? What did we gain methodologically? What would be the obvious next steps? Several considerations arose that we shall address briefly here:

First, we came to the conclusion it would be advantageous to involve scholars from several more disciplines. Their prospective contribution could considerably enrich the breadth of the solutions. Especially professionals specialized in musicology or performance studies, fields used to tackling the challenges raised by ephemeral phenomena, could make seminal contributions.[19] As it is closely aligned to the concept of a musical score, we would like to mention Richard Rinehart's approach for digital and media art forms – including Internet art or software art – as a further promising path worth exploring in its scope. Like comparable approaches (PANIC, Brisbane; CMCM, V2 Rotterdam etc.) his Media Art Notation System (MANS, UC berkeley) is a descriptive framework based on XML as an expression format and on the Digital Item Dec-

19 Cf. for instance: Gabriella Giannachi & Jonah Westerman (eds.): Histories of performance documentation. Museum, artistic, and scholarly practices. London 2018; Michael J.H. Woolley: Documenting performance art. Documentation in practice. In: International Journal of Performance Arts and Digital Media, vol. 10, no. 1, 2014, pp. 48-66; Pip Laurenson & Vivian E.J.P. van Saaze: Collecting Performance-based Art. New Challenges and Shifting Perspectives. In: Outi Remes, Laura McCulloch & Marika Leino (eds.): Performativity in the Gallery. Staging Interactive Encounters. Oxford 2013, pp. 27-41.

laration Language (DIDL). While Rinehart considers the code also as being a kind of score, he sets out to develop something 'universal' and language or platform independent, akin to a musical score. He foresees three levels of implementation all of which are supposed to be machine-processable: from general to very fine-grained descriptions. Rinehart aims to produce notations on media art works on such a "level of detail necessary not just to describe the works but to recreate them."[20] This links his endeavour to the profession of preservationists which it would also be obvious to include: LIMA's symposium *Transformation Digital Art 2021* resulted in three collaborative workshop summaries discussing strategies for the documentation of media art works as there is still no standard solution for this task. All the case studies led to a recreation of the respective artwork, which informed the documentation and is beyond the scope of this article.[21] The strategy by Centre Pompidou, for instance, included the extraction of code into a human-readable pdf or even visual maps of the artwork's interactive parts in a classification that was designed to be understood quickly and visually.

Second, it turned out to be very likely that there were different expectations and views not only on a phenomenological level, but also regarding what to find on the source code level. It may be profitable to run a follow-up experiment of parallelised analyses by different code-literate scholars that focus on this particular part of a browser.

Third, the question arose as to what to do practically with the rich variety of paths taken. The experiment was revealing. Although it is neither practical nor feasible to generate a whole variety of documentations for each individual browser, it is not completely beyond the scope of the project either: on a smaller scale, a hybrid method combining four+ different

20 Richard Rinehart: The Media Art Notation System. Documenting and Preserving Digital/Media Art. In: Leonardo, vol. 40, no. 2, 2007, pp. 181–187, here: p. 183.

21 LIMA: Transformation Digital Art 2021. Symposium 24.–26.3.2021, https://www.li-ma.nl/lima/article/transformation-digital-art-2021 [accessed 28.3.2022].

views (the artist, two scholars, and 'the audience') of one artwork, was elaborated by Lizzie Muller and Caitlin Jones in 2007 during their collaboration at Fondation Langlois.[22] Their focus on the artist's intention as well as the audience response allowed them to address the possible tension between expectations and factual experiences.

There are arguments for and against unifying as many facets of the different approaches as possible. With the prospect of providing the documentation results in a database[23], a compromise could be to bring all the approaches to a formalized level and to conceive the many steps as modules in a possibility space of methods. Each person engaged in the documentation could then still work according to their individual preferences and abilities, but by checking boxes for the methodological modules they integrated, each documentation would gain transparency through added meta data.

Fourth, and related to the previous idea, was the question of the degree to which the different approaches taken would actually be formalisable and could be formulated as prescriptive steps everybody could adopt. Astonishingly, Inge Hinterwaldner, who always saw her contribution as being among the most unstructured approaches (her self-perceived meanderings are clearly depicted in Fig. 1 on page 98), and the contribution by Henrik Wache, Sarah Hönigsberg and Barbara Dinter as being the most structured (expressed in Table 1 [p. 110]), seemed to find common ground in the discussion. The scholars from the area of business information systems found the image theoretician's way of exploring the browser as being very similar to what they did before then formalising their steps. What first seemed to be the extremes of a range now turned out to be possible consecutive stages of investigation. This led to reflections on what requirements

22 Caitlin Jones, Lizzie Muller & David Rokeby: The Giver of Names (1991-). Documentary Collection. Introduction to the Collection. In: La Foundation Daniel Langlois, 2008, https://www.fondation-langlois.org/html/e/page.php?NumPage=2121 [accessed 1.4.2022].

23 Cf. Dušan Barok et al.: Archiving Complex Digital Artworks. In: Journal of the Institute of Conservation, vol. 42, no. 2, 2019, 94-113.

must be met in order to work towards a set of generalisable instructions. Unlike all other contributions, Hinterwaldner's narration included setting up a series of test arrangements that were prepared for improved visibility of the performative outcome, executed, evaluated, and eventually repeated. Some of the test ideas could be generalisable and transferrable to other applications, for instance the comparison between the HTML-code of a website as seen in the source code viewer of a commercial browser with its appearance in artistic browsers; or the analysis of the sound events. She and Wache et al. share a relatively open approach to gathering information about the browser. Furthermore, these are the only contributions to provide labels for addressing and capsuling the findings.

Since not all contributions were based on such a series of 'system tests', they do seem to have different degrees of affinity to and compatibility with the Wache et al. approach due to their chosen focus. One further crucial aspect regarding how easily findings can be fused into one structure, has to do with how strongly they are rooted in an individual sensation or a specific theory building which needs to remain attached as a pretext.

DOI: 10.5282/ubm/epub.93522

Acknowledgements

We express our deep gratitude to the artists Joan Heemskerk and Dirk Paesmans for supporting our research by granting us valuable insights into their art production and by providing us with their code. Also, we would like to thank our contributors for agreeing to participate in this collective experiment. We are aware that the task we gave them was somewhat out of the ordinary. During the process of developing the experimental setup, the trial carried out by our colleague Erna Fiorentini and her feedback drew our attention to several important aspects. We are grateful for her contribution. Finally, our thanks go towards the German Science Foundation (DFG), the institution that funded this research within the realm of the Priority Program *Das digitale Bild* (2019–2022).

Biographies

Edited by
Inge Hinterwaldner
Daniela Hönigsberg
Konstantin Mitrokhov

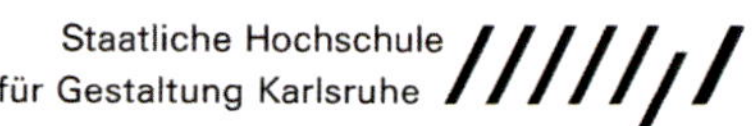

DFG-Schwerpunktprogramm ‚Das digitale Bild'
Projekt Browserkunst. Navigieren mit Stil

Erstveröffentlichung: 2022
Gestaltung und Satz: Lydia Kähny und Sophie Ramm

Diese Publikation wurde finanziert durch die Deutsche Forschungsgemeinschaft.
München, Open Publishing LMU

DOI 10.5282/ubm/epub.93518
ISBN 978-3-487-16315-4
Library of Congress Control Number
Die Deutsche Nationalbibliothek verzeichnet diese Publikation in der Deutschen Nationalbibliografie; detaillierte bibliografische Daten sind abrufbar unter http://dnb.dnb.de

Reihe: Begriffe des digitalen Bildes
Reihenherausgeber
Hubertus Kohle
Hubert Locher

Zeitfracht Medien GmbH
Ferdinand-Jühlke-Straße 7
99095 Erfurt, Deutschland
produktsicherheit@kolibri360.de